POWER
TO WITNESS

The Story of Charles Beach

POWER TO WITNESS

How the Holy Spirit Inspires Personal Witnessing

Peggy Scarborough
With Lois Beach

Unless otherwise indicated, Scripture quotations are taken from the King James Version of the Bible.

Scripture quotations marked *NIV* are taken from the *Holy Bible, New International Version®*. *NIV®*. Copyright © 1973, 1978, 1984 by International Bible Society. Used by permission of Zondervan Publishing House. All rights reserved.

Scripture quotations marked *NKJV* are taken from the *New King James Version.* Copyright © 1979, 1980, 1982, 1990, 1995, Thomas Nelson Inc., Publishers.

Book Editor:	Wanda Griffith
Editorial Assistant:	Tammy Hatfield
Copy Editors:	Esther Metaxas
	Cresta Shawver
	Oreeda Burnette
Inside Layout:	R. Ariel Vázquez

Library of Congress Catalog Card Number: 2002106843
ISBN: 0-87148-494-3
Copyright © 2002 by Pathway Press
Cleveland, Tennessee 37311
All Rights Reserved
Printed in the United States of America

DEDICATION

To

Sharlinda Beach Turner, M.D.,

the daughter of Charles and Lois Beach,
and her daughters,

Cindy and *Christa Turner.*

Charles said they were like the little prince
in the French classic *Le Petit Prince,*
by Antoine de Saint-Exupery.
They "sunshine" the house.

CONTENTS

ACKNOWLEDGMENTS

Charles Beach was the greatest personal soulwinner I have ever known. It has been a great thrill to write his story and work with his wonderful wife, Lois Underwood Beach. Lois Beach is one of the most brilliant women in the body of Christ today. She is a family person, a scholar, a researcher and a great woman of God. She has been my friend for years. I love her.

As at all times, and especially while writing this book, I was made aware of my desperate need for the illumination, guidance and energizing of the Holy Spirit. I have also felt very dependent on the prayers of others to complete this project.

I am greatly indebted to my precious husband, Neigel L. Scarborough. Without his willing and able assistance, along with his love and patience, this project would not have been accomplished.

I appreciate Dr. Dan Boling, Dr. Bill George, Wanda Griffith and Tammy Hatfield for the many hours they worked to complete this project.

My sincere thanks to Leonard Albert, Dr. T.L. Lowery, Dr. Don Aultman, Mitch Maloney, Ray Sanders, Doug LeRoy, Bob Blackaby, John Lombard, Betty Robbins, Martha Wong, Glenna Lee, Wanda Fox, Lorraine Carroll, Helen Anderson, Gerald Johnson, Bill Wooten, Rich Ussery, Phil Higgins, Randy Hamon, and the many other former students and associates who shared their memories of this great man of God.

Dr. Beach wrote an article for the *Evangel*, June 10, 1965, titled "I Remember the Church of God Lay Witnessing Movement." In it he listed a cadre of student workers:

Samuel Stanley, Betty Shewmaker Call, Marlene De Fino Starr, Luther Hobbs, Gisella Hanke Hathaway, Larry Walt, Carolyn Baldwin, Carolyn and Curley Walters, Fred Brannon, Minuard Ashemore, Bob and Irene Cox, John Daniel, J.C. Gaston, Ollie Lee, Troy Baggett, and others whose names escaped him. They were all faithful to hold street services, jail services, child evangelism classes, church-in-the-home meetings, and outreach Sunday school classes in the mid and late 1950s.

In his article, Charles remembered two great lady preachers, Rose Douglas and Frances Carden, whose touching sermons in county and local jails melted the hearts of many hardened prisoners. He also recalled some great street preachers: James Allen, Bob Lyons and the late Bobby Sustar.

G.A. Swanson and Harold Snyder conducted the first weekend PFC invasion; Terry Beavers and Bill Wooten developed the PFC house-to-house witnessing program; and Ray Sanders, Aubrey Maye, Gerald Johnson, Douglas LeRoy, Bob Blackaby, Bill George, Dickie Davis, Lenny Walls, Douglas Slocumb, Edsel Hand, Rich Ussery and Ted Gee led summer witness teams to all parts of the United States and overseas. Because of their ministry, 15 new Church of God congregations were started.

He recalled how Betty Robbins Standifer, Linda Johnson Harvard, Martha Smith Wong, Mary Margaret Holdman Morris, Margie Johnson Walls, Lorraine Carroll, the late Karen Lilly Conine, the late Darlene Herndon, Shelvry Hendren, Glenna Sheppard Lee, and the late Sara Conn Wesson had fruitful witnessing ministries and proved that God's greatest work—soulwinning (Luke 19:10)—also included dedicated lady workers.

He remembered the great preaching of many of the PFC members—John Lombard, Harmon Roberts, Jerome Mueller, Steven Conn, and one of the most innovative of PFC leaders, Howard Hancock.

He personally observed the work of some of the most effective one-to-one witnesses: Dr. Esdras Betancourt, Pat Peters Albert, David Barnes, Keith Black, and the efforts of Willie Lawrence to get the gospel "to the Jew first."

He recalled the late R. Leonard Carroll, who, as president of Lee College, made possible the first house-to-house witnessing instructions for the PFC club. He appreciated Rufus Platt, who supported the infant program through its early growth.

He appreciated Wade Horton and Paul Henson, who, as state leaders, gave the Lee College group its first out-of-state invitation to Mississippi.

He remembered Don Aultman, who—along with Cecil Knight, L.H. Aultman and Ray H. Hughes—developed PFC's national and international summer witnessing programs in which Dr. Beach personally participated with Lee College students.

His appreciation for Dr. Ray H. Hughes was great. He remembered his leadership from 1960 to 1966 that brought the student-witnessing program to its full flowering—reaching 84,000 homes in 1963 and '64. As General Overseer in 1972, Dr. Hughes opened the first office of Lay Affairs, utilizing personnel who had gained broad experience in the Lee College campus program.

He remembered Ralph Williams, who, as chairman of the National Evangelism Board, gave the witnessing program its first official recognition; Walter Pettitt, who, as the first national evangelism director, fully supported the transition of lay witnessing from a campus program to a churchwide endeavor involving laity of all ages and talents; T.L. Lowery who pastored the North Cleveland Church of God and furnished the arena to test and develop the many in-church and outreach lay ministries; George Alford and Bob Blazier, state evangelism directors, who provided the first broad opportunities on the field for Lay Affairs office personnel to implement their concepts to this church's army of Spirit-filled laity.

He remembered C.R. Spain, national evangelism director, who guided the lay affairs office through its earliest efforts.

He recalled Houston Morehead, the first director of Men's Fellowship, who got the lay movement off the ground by chartering the first local men's fellowship in the late 1960s and Bill Sheeks, evangelism director of North Carolina, who was the first state leader to charter over 100—and later over 200—local Men's Fellowship groups.

He remembered John Nichols, who introduced the Lay Affairs office to the most productive program of lay witnessing ever developed in this country—Evangelism Explosion. Seeing the effectiveness of the training in lay seminars and impact rallies, Dr. Nichols worked with Dr. Beach and Leonard Albert, and forged and inaugurated the most effective and far-reaching lay-training effort ever to surface in the history of this church—the Schools of Lay Evangelism.

Dr. Beach remembered Raymond Crowley, the national evangelism director, who made it possible for laymen in mission states, including Alaska and Hawaii, to be introduced to effective lay-witnessing projects. He put forth enormous efforts to develop state and local lay services to men and women in correctional institutions all across America.

There were many other people who followed those I've listed here. There are hundreds of people who could be listed here. We would have liked to have included many other experiences, but time and space prohibited it. Please forgive us if we did not mention your name and you were involved with this great soulwinning endeavor. It was not intentional.

As you read the following pages, may you be inspired as never before to win the lost at any cost.

—Peggy Scarborough

TRIBUTE TO A MOST UNUSUAL MAN

During my first semester at Lee in 1960, I met Charles Beach. I immediately observed that he was a most unusual man. *Webster's Dictionary* defines unusual as *"not ordinary, uncommon, and rare."* These words truly describe this man who has been my unusual, faithful friend for almost 40 years.

Unusual in the most mannerly way he demonstrated his love for Lois, his wife, and Sharlinda, his daughter . . .

Unusual in that he was very selective in whom he let drive his coddled car, especially on PFC invasions . . .

Unusual in that he always gave tribute to others when he should have been the recipient . . .

Unusual in his ability to make us laugh through his jokes and impersonations . . .

Unusual in his care and concern for those in the hospitals and nursing homes . . .

Unusual in his ability to recall people, time, places and events most of us have forgotten . . .

Unusual in making others feel they were someone special and they could do great things for God . . .

Unusual in his teaching ability . . .

Unusual in his stewardship, in the way he always helped others financially . . .

Unusual in that he could go days without a good night of rest . . .

Unusual in that he persistently followed up on everyone . . .

Unusual in his burden to train leaders for witnessing and leading lost men to Christ . . .

Unusual in his skillful communications . . .

Unusual in his knowledge of Mormonism and Jehovah's Witnesses, often knowing more about their beliefs then they themselves . . .

Unusual in that he was always putting others ahead of himself . . .

Unusual in his fervor for a personal, constant Christian lifestyle . . .

Unusual in his self-sacrificing . . .

Unusual in his perpetual prayer life . . .

Unusual in his testimony . . .

Unusual in his desire to win everyone to Christ without prejudice . . .

Unusual in that his life has possibly influenced more men and women for Christ than any other single man in the Church of God . . .

And on a more personal note . . .

Unusual in that he has kept Kathy and me, our three daughters and their families in his prayer journal for these 40 years.

Unusual in that he had faith in me and asked me to preach in a jail service. Later he asked me to go on the first PFC summer witnessing team to the city of Providence, Rhode Island. Because of the unwavering faith of this man, my life has truly been enriched. I will always be indebted to Charles R. Beach.

We love you Brother Beach.

—Ray and Kathy Sanders

FOREWORD

I have always believed in the sovereignty of God, and only God could pull off something like this. Toward the end of World War II, an unsaved sailor from Texas finds Christ on a transport ship after fighting many battles for months at sea in the Pacific theater. After the war, he comes to Lee University (then Lee College) and eventually ends up teaching at the school. From the beginning, he is involved in personal evangelism. He trains thousands of kids at the school on how to lead a soul to Christ.

After graduation, one of those students, a pretty girl by the name of Teresa Peters, returns to her native state of Maine and leads her boss (also a former sailor) to Christ. He receives the baptism of the Holy Spirit after reading a booklet written by that same professor. He then decides to attend Lee University, and providentially meets that same teacher after a local church service. They form a ministry partnership that lasts for 30 years. We travel to many parts of the world and together teach hundreds of thousands of people how to witness and reach the lost. Well, I promise that's just how it happened, and it happened to me.

God must have ordained that Brother Charles Beach and I work together. It was such a natural fit from the beginning. He was always the teacher and I the student—eager to learn. I knew in principle that every Christian was a minister, but Brother Beach taught it in practice. Outside of Jesus I have never met a better soulwinner than this bigger-than- life layman from Texas. He taught me how to win souls and teach others to do the same. He taught me that I could do something significant for Christ without ministerial credentials. He taught me to love the church—

the local church, the Church of God denomination, and the church universal. He taught me how to speak before people. He taught me humor. I once said to him, "When you die, I don't want your money; I just want that box full of jokes that you keep in the back of your Rambler."

Well, many years before his passing, he gave me that box. I have cherished it and, believe me, I have used its contents thousands of times. He taught me the value of prayer and Bible study by consistently displaying these traits in his personal lifestyle. He taught me how to be a better husband and father through his unending love and admiration for his wife and only child, a lovely daughter (same as me).

Yes, Charles R. Beach was quite the teacher. He helped me get my first job as a lay director of evangelism in a local church. He also helped me get my second and only other job in the church working with the Department of Lay Ministries. I have been doing that for 28 years.

Back in Maine in 1968 when I first fell in love with Jesus (and Teresa Peters), I read a book titled *Beloved of the Chinese,* by another one of Brother Beach's "students," Miss Peggy Humphrey. I was fascinated with this book and it really helped me to grow in Christ. This lady also taught at Lee University and was very much involved with the witnessing efforts. She has always had an outstanding ability to tell a story in words. She's still at it today and now, as Dr. Peggy Humphrey Scarborough, she writes this most wonderful narrative of the life and ministry of this great legend of our time. You will enjoy this book because it is all true . . . and it provides great inspiration.

—Leonard C. Albert
Director of Lay Ministries

PREFACE

Charles Beach had love and great respect for his mentor Dr. Ray H. Hughes. Charles often said, "Ray Hughes is a Biblical scholar. I go to him when I have a Biblical question." Dr. Hughes encouraged Charles to research the Scripture. Charles Beach believed the Scriptures provide answers and solutions to the problems we face in life today regardless of our age, philosophy, or background.

I would like to express deep appreciation to Dr. Peggy Scarborough, who captured on paper the life story of Charles Beach—his military career; sense of humor; love for magic, music and languages; and his desire "to win the lost at any cost" to Jesus Christ.

I knew Charles could care less about his life story ever being told, even though it was uniquely filled with the unexpected; but he had some "golden nuggets" on the Holy Spirit he had researched for years that he desired to be published before his death. Now, more than a year after his passing, the Lord has provided a way for me to honor my husband's last wish—to help others understand the Holy Spirit.

A note of thanks is due Dr. Paul Conn, president of Lee University, for the example he set for the faculty, staff and student body. He made it clear that an excellent education was important; but also, that a deep spiritual understanding of the Scriptures was necessary for a successful Christian life. Paul Conn was and is a leader— one with whom you can joke, laugh, disagree, argue and still maintain a high degree of respect for each other.

My respect and appreciation go to Pastor Mitch Maloney of the North Cleveland Church of God and to Leonard Albert, director of the Department of Lay Ministries, for continuing the work that was an integral part of my husband's life.

I must also express gratitude, love and respect for my daughter, Sharlinda, who is always there for me with her strength, compassion, understanding and Christian attitude. Her love for her father made his life an eternal joy.

—Dr. Lois Underwood Beach

⚡ PART ONE ⚡

THE CHARLES BEACH STORY

1

PREPARATION OF
A GREAT HERO

"God is preparing His heroes; and when the opportune moment comes, He will put them in their places in a moment, and the world will wonder where they came from." This quote from missionary Paul C. Pitt describes the life of Charles Beach. God prepared this great hero for the Church of God's soul-winning endeavors. He lit a fire that will never go out.

Bombs were exploding. It was World War II. The place was Iwo Jima. The ship was the USS Callaghan (DD 792). Inside the ship a frightening stillness made the crewmen aware of every sound and movement. They were terror-stricken. Charles was the commander's yeoman on this destroyer. He had served on other destroyers—the USS Porterfield (DD 682) and the USS Irwin. Charles had been in 30 Pacific combat landings. Most recently, they had been in air battles with Japanese airplanes. Six of his fleet's ships had already been hit and three had been sunk, killing all his buddies.

Being a yeoman on a destroyer was a serious assignment. Destroyers were originally designed to launch torpedo attacks on the enemy fleet. The destroyer had large torpedo tubes to launch the 3,841-pound steel monsters at the enemy.

Suddenly enemy shells struck his own ship. The commander sent Charles to tell the gunnery crew to continue shooting. He crawled over the dead bodies of many of his comrades. This was the most horrible experience he had ever encountered in his life. Depression hit him as never before. He had to go up a set of stairs to get to the gun crew. At the top of the stairs, he stood up and stared straight into the enemy's large gun. The shell was advancing straight toward him. There was no time to run. He knew he was dead. But God must have sent an angel. Looking behind him, Charles saw that part of the wall was blown away right where he was standing. "It had to go through me to get there," he later said, "but I wasn't killed." Charles later shared, "To this day I don't understand it, unless God had a work for me to do." And what a work God had planned for him. What a life!

Charles suddenly realized the fragility of life. He did not want to die, because he knew he was lost. He was not even injured—maybe because he prayed. But many of his friends were injured and many others killed. Those who lived knew God had spared the life of Charles Beach.

Thoughts raced through his mind like a swift stream. *What is my purpose in living anyway? If I make it safely back home, can I make a difference? Is there any reason for my being in this terrible battle? Was there really a purpose for my being born? Do I have a future? If I were to die on this ocean, where would I go? Would anyone know I had lived?*

Charles Beach had joined the army in 1942, after World War II had started in December 1941. He was sent to San Diego for basic training and served a year of shore duty there. Then he decided he did not like the ground forces and transferred to the Navy, where he stayed aboard destroyers and subchasers for more than three years. Sometimes he was gone as much as 10 months without seeing land. He spent 40 months in the Navy.

Little did he know God was preparing him to be a greater military man. Being the commander's yeoman, Charles gained much knowledge in how to get people to do what they needed to do. On one occasion the captain sent him to another ship with a message. When he arrived, he saluted the officer in charge. With a sneer, the officer said, "And whose little boy are you?" When Charles returned to the commander's office, he told his commanding officer of the insulting experience. The commander was infuriated. He sent for the officer and set him straight, yelling, "Listen to me, Officer! Yeoman Charles Beach represented me. I sent my representative. With my authority behind him, he was as if he were head of the fleet." That officer made a gracious apology. From this, Charles learned the authority of the power of attorney, as well as the chain of command. He learned that in the service of the Lord, you have authority when you represent the Commander in Chief. Perhaps he also picked up some authoritarian skills, which he later used with Lee College Pioneers for Christ to help them become good soldiers of the Cross.

Charles prayed. His prayers came from fear and confusion. But the God who was preparing him to be a greater soldier heard him anyway. This attack at sea began the story of the great anointing of one of God's greatest warriors.

Memories of Childhood Days

Like many people who face danger, Charles' thoughts carried him back to his childhood. When he was younger, he had occasionally attended a Methodist Episcopal Church. Although he was sprinkled at age 10, he had no concept of salvation or how to attain heaven.

Born October 23, 1922, in Stephenville (a small town near Fort Worth), Texas, Charles was the youngest of seven children, four of whom died in infancy. Only Charles and his two sisters survived. When Charles was only 10 years of age, his father, a blacksmith, died leaving only him, his mother and two sisters. Because Charles was so small, his mother did not allow him to go to school until he was 8 years old. His mother worked hard to provide for her family. Charles was close to his two sisters, Audrey and Lola, and their sons Bill Dorsey and Jerry Shugart. Throughout his life, Charles referred to his Texas family with much affection, including his cousins.

Charles' first job at age 11 was delivering papers. He had to get up before daylight to deliver papers before going to school. Then he got a job working for Western Union. In 1938, he got a job delivering letters, but when he lost one, he was fired. He felt like a failure! But this was all in the plan of God for the making of a great leader for the church.

Charles was versatile. He had a real ear for music and joined a harmonica band called "The Harmonica Harmony Boys." They had a regular radio program. He participated in debates, Future Farmers of America, and became an avid stamp and coin collector. He also developed an interest in magic. As a child he would hitchhike to Dallas to attend performances of great magicians. He figured out every trick the Great Blackstone did, except two. Even in his later years, his daughter bought tickets for the family to the David Copperfield Magic Show in Chattanooga. Even after all these years, Charles figured out all the tricks except one. Little did he know then that God had a plan for even his own magic acts. Through the years, magic paved the way for Charles to share the gospel with thousands of children.

Memories of Teenage and Young-Adult Years

In some areas of his life, failure became a pattern for Charles. Through the ninth grade he was an average student. But in the 10th grade, feeling he had reached an insurmountable obstacle, he dropped out of school because of pressure from a heavy workload. But he had a strong determination and kept telling himself, "You can make it! You can make it!" Later he knew God was preparing him for the time when he could help his students conquer insurmountable obstacles.

He took a job in the post office delivering mail and telegrams, but soon dropped out to work with the Civilian Conservation Corps in Colorado (President Roosevelt's program for providing jobs for young men). He educated himself in writing and reading skills. During this time he acquired some typing jobs and taught reading and math to illiterate corpsmen.

After Charles became a supervisor, one day while "telling an employee off" because he did not like the way the job was being done, his top administrator walked in. In a loud voice, the administrator reprimanded him, "Beach, let me tell you one thing: There is no one indispensable around here, and that includes you." He was pointing his finger all the time. This was more preparation for teaching Pioneers for Christ students responsibility and accountability.

Then he joined the Navy in 1942.

Soulwinners on a Ship Led Charles Beach to Christ

When Charles boarded the USS Admiral Koontz, a troop ship, on March 19, 1945, to return to the United States, he was filled with confusion. Two Navy buddies invited him to attend a Bible study. During this 19-day trip home, these dedicated young sailors explained clearly and Biblically the plan of salvation. For the first time Charles understood and prayed the sinner's prayer: "Jesus, I am sorry I have sinned. I ask You to forgive me. You said in Your Word, 'If we confess our sins, [You are] faithful and just to forgive us our sins, and to cleanse us from all unrighteousness' (1 John 1:9). I believe You died on the cross for me. If I had been the only lost person in the world, You would have died for me. Now, Jesus, take Your precious blood and wash all my sins away. If You will save me, I'll live for You; and I'll work for You all the days of my life." His buddies made the scripture plain to him: "Him that cometh to me I will in no wise cast out" (John 6:37). Tears flowed down his face. Charles realized that on the authority of God's Word, he was now a new creation. Old things were passed away, and all things were now new (see 2 Corinthians 5:17). What a heaviness was gone! He was free! He had a purpose for living. Fear of death or failure would no longer permeate his thinking.

The Holy Spirit

His buddies also outlined to Charles the purpose of the baptism in the Holy Ghost. These Spirit-filled sailors guided him through practically every important scripture on this God-given power to witness for Christ.

The first night off the ship in San Diego, he and his two Christian friends attended a street service. After the street service, they went into a small mission on Embarcadero Street to pray. Though this was the first Pentecostal service Charles had ever attended, he received the Holy Spirit baptism, with the evidence of speaking in tongues. Here Charles received a power that paved the way for the rest of his life. His experience was not just one of "Bless me, Lord." His thoughts from that day until the end of his life were, "Make me a blessing." These few days charted the course for one of the most dynamic soulwinners who ever lived. Little did those sailors know to whom they were giving the Word of Life.

The next day a non-Pentecostal attempted to show Charles that the Spirit baptism with the Bible evidence of speaking in tongues was no longer valid. He argued with Charles that "tongues have ceased." But he was too late. Charles had already had a personal experience. Also, those sailors had given him such supportive scriptures that no one could make him doubt his experience; the Word of God was already in him.

Proper Preparation

The man who led Charles to the Lord taught him the discipline of systematic Bible study. This proved to be the hallmark for Charles for the rest of his life. Whatever he taught, he could back up with scores of scriptures. He was dedicated to Bible study. He loved it. He "ate" the Word of God daily.

How to Win the Lost

During the time Charles was enrolled in a Navy school in San Diego, he gained experience in working in missions. Shortly afterward, he was transferred to San Pedro, California, where he attended a Foursquare Gospel church. He met a number of students from L.I.F.E. Bible School who took him to jail services, street meetings and mission meetings—involving him in many forms of personal evangelism. Something got into his spirit. He loved winning the lost. There was nothing in life that excited him like seeing people come to Jesus.

After Charles got out of the Navy in 1945, he returned to his home in Texas and joined the Church of God in 1946. His friend Glen Maxwell, a student from L.I.F.E. Bible College, who had influenced Charles greatly, also came to Texas. He and Charles traveled from town to town, holding street meetings. This was a wonderful experience, but then Glen got married and moved to another state.

His pastor, Leslie Winnegar, and his youth director, Manuel Campbell, tried to influence him to become a preacher, but Charles felt so unsuccessful. It wasn't for him. Again that feeling of failure came over him. But a gnawing feeling inside convinced Charles that God had another ministry for him.

Pastor Winnegar knew God had His hand on Charles and insisted that he attend Bible Training School (BTS) in Sevierville, Tennessee. His pastor said, "Charles, if you don't go to Lee College, you will never amount to anything in the world." So Charles passed the GED test, applied for his VA benefits under the GI Bill, and enrolled in Bible Training School in Sevierville.

A College Student Meets His Wife

Charles arrived on the campus with cowboy boots, dungarees and a guitar. He had on a long-sleeved white shirt with the words embroidered in large black letters, "Jesus is coming soon." He had another one embroidered with the words, "Jesus Saves" in red. Soon he met a beautiful young home economics teacher. The first time he saw her he thought, *She is a pretty one.* He did not even know her name.

Lois Underwood was a popular teacher. Many of the male students enrolled in her home economics class to learn etiquette. The textbook was *Boys Will Be Men.* They enjoyed the charm of the beautiful and gracious young teacher. Because she loved her job, Lois never woke up in the morning without looking forward to her work. Some of her students were Don Aultman, Eddie Williams, Bennie Triplett, Harry Whittington, Harold Lucas and Calvin Newton, men who would become leaders in the Church of God. However, Charles did not enroll in this course.

Couples who wanted to leave campus had to have a chaperone. The students could get someone to go along with the chaperone as an escort, probably to keep them from having to entertain the chaperone. A group of students wanted Miss Underwood for a chaperone, so they asked Charles to go along with her. He said, "No thanks!

I'll make my own dates." Then when he learned who she was, he apologized and asked her to go out with him.

As a preacher's daughter and one of 12 children, Lois did not want to marry a preacher. Little did she know she was falling in love with someone who would be more actively involved in ministry than any preacher she had ever known.

They married a year later, August 30, 1947. This had to be one of those marriages made in heaven. Charles, later in life, said: "My wife, Lois Underwood Beach, is a continual and immense encouragement to my personal endeavors. She is the unsung heroine in and the primary reason for the successes that have come my way." She was always a stabilizing force in Charles' life. When the discouraging times came, she kept him going. Later in life he declared, "We still have a romance going."

"He never put any pressure on me, even for cooking and cleaning," said Lois. "He always did his own clothes." There were more important things to do for God than spending hours in a kitchen cooking or cleaning. His idea of a wife was bigger than that. Charles never forgot an anniversary, a birthday, a holiday, or any special event in the family. He was always giving her flowers and gifts. They did not have a lot of money, but Lois had the best perfumes Paris had to offer. He always opened his wife's door when entering or leaving his car. He got her coat and her chair, held her hand often, and took her out to eat for a date practically every night he was in town. Sometimes it was just for a sandwich, but it was a meaningful time. Charles always had a low tolerance for any man who did not appreciate his wife and treat her as a gentleman.

The Birthing of a Scholar

After graduating from Lee College in Cleveland, Tennessee (the school had moved to Cleveland and changed its name), in 1948 with an associate of arts degree, Charles continued his education at the University of Tennessee in Knoxville, where he received a bachelor of arts degree in foreign languages. After he and Lois spent a summer of study in France, he began his master's program in French and Spanish in 1949.

While working on his master's degree and teaching at Lee College for one week, he was called into active duty during the Korean conflict in the summer of 1950. Although, he was stationed in Charleston, South Carolina, he was on a ship for months at a time. When he could get a furlough, he would hitchhike back to Cleveland to see Lois, who was pregnant. They did not have the money to buy a car or even a bus ticket. Their daughter, Sharlinda, was born in a Navy hospital in Charleston, South Carolina, on September 15, 1951.

Jehovah-Jireh Always Came Through

When Charles was finally released from the service, he returned to the University of Tennessee to complete his studies.

These were years of trial, but blessing. Because Charles was a full-time student, they lived on Lois' salary of $150 a month for nine months of the year. During the summer months when they had no income, Cooke's Grocery and Central Drug Store let them charge their groceries and medicine. It took an entire year to pay them back, but their needs were met.

Almost Missing the Will of God

Charles had such a burning zeal to work for God. He wanted to tell the world "Jesus saves." Learning of the need for a missionary in Haiti, Charles seemed to be the perfect candidate. He had a great love for all the people of the world, and since he spoke French, he could pick up any dialect. So he was approached by members of the World Missions Department to become a missionary to Haiti.

Lois was positive God had called her to Lee College. The thought of leaving Lee was disappointing, but when the World Missions Board asked Lois how she felt, she responded, "If my husband feels God has called him to the mission field in Haiti, I will gladly go."

A few days later, the field representative for World Missions was preaching at North Cleveland Church of God. At the end of his message, he asked, "Is there anybody who feels a burning desire to go to the mission field?" Charles stood to his feet. The minister voiced, "Yes, Brother Beach, I know your heart." Then he asked, "How many others would be willing to go if God called you?" Lois leaped to her feet. She was willing to go if Charles told her he was called of God to go. With love and submission, she said, "Charles, God brought us together. If it is God's will for us to be together, we must have the same feelings." Charles' reply was, "I am not really called to be a missionary either. I just want to win the lost of the world to Jesus and I enjoy the French language. It would be a great experience for me." That was it. He did not go to Haiti. They both realized they were called to Lee College.

For two years Charles taught at the University of Tennessee in Knoxville. Then in 1954 he joined the Lee College faculty. He later turned down a permanent teaching position at the University of Tennessee, because he wanted to work for God at Lee College. He had a dream for the school.

2

TURNING A COLLEGE INTO AN ARMY

Leland Smelser wrote these words: "Since 1956, Charles Beach and his students have turned street corners into chapels, porches into sanctuaries, and converted shopping malls into worship centers and Christian literature distribution points. From a small, secluded office at Lee College, without the advantage of position or the benefits of officialdom, this layman lit a flame of evangelism that has consumed the hearts of thousands of ministers and members. As a yielded vessel, this one man challenged a college, then an entire denomination to become a soulwinning church."

Charles Beach came back to Lee College in 1954. A small organization called Youth for Christ had been started by Priscilla Odom in the late 1940s, but had declined after her departure. Periodically the group conducted street services and jail services. In 1956 Charles began working with the group. When he saw Sue Hosch and Josephine Kon going door-to-door witnessing, he became convicted of his sin of omission. He repented before the Lord: "God, I have failed to teach and preach Jesus Christ in every house. Make me a soulwinner." He did not associate with this group to build a program—he simply wanted to work for God. That was all! Soon Charles felt he had a mandate from the Lord to lead these students into personal soulwinning. He followed the Savior's example, who had sent the disciples out two by two into every city and place and said to them, "Behold, I give you power to tread on serpents and scorpions, and over all the power of the enemy: and nothing shall by any means hurt you" (Luke 10:19).

One day Charles overheard a remark made by a student, Luther Johnson, who said, "I'm going home to work for God. There's nothing in school for a Christian to do to work for the Lord." That settled it. He had to motivate these students to work for God. Shortly he had them conducting street services and going to the jails and poverty-stricken areas to witness.

He began preaching soulwinning to every potential soulwinner on campus. He reminded them that after converting the Samaritan woman at the well, Jesus said to His disciples, "Say not ye, There are yet four months, and then cometh harvest? behold, I say unto you, Lift up your eyes, and look on the fields; for they are white already to harvest" (John 4:35).

The following material written by Charles was published in the *Encyclopedia on Evangelism*. He taught it to his students.

How to Lead a Soul to Christ

You can witness to, and lead a soul to Christ if you will follow this simple formula:

After prayer, approach an individual in a sensible, sincere and tactful manner—at work, at school, on the street or in a home. Strike up a conversation on any subject of mutual interest, such as the weather, eminent people or world events. The Lord has left us an excellent example for this particular approach in His dealing with the Samaritan woman at the well in John 4. Do not do all the talking, but guide the conversation.

Next, focus the conversation on the individual you hope to win to Christ. Ask him about his health. If he is looking well, comment on that fact, thanking the Lord for his good health. If he is not well, ask him about his illness.

Then bring up questions that will eventually lead to your finding out whether or not he is saved. "Do you go to church? Which church do you attend? Do you attend Sunday school?" Regardless of his response, he is now on the subject of his soul. You may now ask these questions: "Are you saved? Have you accepted Christ as your Savior? Have you repented of and confessed your sins? Are you daily confessing Christ as your Lord?"

If the individual answers yes to these questions and has met these conditions (believing, confessing, repenting, witnessing), then you can assume he is saved. If he claims to be saved and indicates that he is not a witness, you may ask him the question Paul asked the disciples at Ephesus: "Have ye received the Holy Ghost since ye believed?" (Acts 19:2). Point out that the Baptism of the Holy Ghost gives one power to witness for Christ (1:8).[1]

The Conversion

If the individual indicates that he has not accepted Christ, you may point him to salvation through the use of four simple scriptures:

1. Believe—"Believe on the Lord Jesus Christ, and thou shalt be saved, and thy house" (Acts 16:31).

2. Confess—"If we confess our sins, he is faithful and just to forgive us our sins, and to cleanse us from all unrighteousness" (1 John 1:9).

3. Repent (turn from sin)—"Except ye repent, ye shall all likewise perish" (Luke 13:3).

4. Witness (confess Christ before men)—"If thou shalt confess with thy mouth the Lord Jesus, and shalt believe in thine heart that God hath raised him from the dead, thou shalt be saved" (Romans 10:9).

Then encourage the individual to pray the sinner's prayer: "Father in heaven, I confess to You that I am a sinner, that I am in need of a Savior in order to inherit eternal life and to escape hell. I do here and now accept Your Son, Jesus the Christ, as my own personal Savior, and ask that His blood cleanse me from all sin."

If he confesses his sins, God will forgive him and cleanse him (1 John 1:9); you will have led another soul to our Lord and Savior, Jesus Christ.

The newly converted Christian must be encouraged to . . .

• Be baptized.

• Read his Bible daily. Have him start with the Book of Acts and the Gospel of John.

• Pray daily, even if it is only for a few moments.

• Testify to the saving power of Jesus. Advise him to tell his friends and family about his conversion.

• Attend Sunday school and church. Point out that church fellowship will help him to grow in grace.

The Follow-Up

Follow-up work with a new convert is probably the weakest area in modern Christendom. Begin this follow-up task by placing in the hands of the new convert two informative tracts: "You Are Now Saved" and "Power to Witness for Christ." A set of five Bible lessons for adults and a separate set for children have been prepared by members of the Lee College Pioneers for Christ for new converts. These lessons may be obtained from the Department of Lay Ministries and are included in this book.

Do not fail to visit the new convert and aid him in every way possible. If possible, arrange a weekly Bible study (using the PFC Bible lessons). The Word is a barrier against the Enemy and sin: "Thy word have I hid in mine heart, that I might not sin against thee" (Psalm 119:11).

One writer has stated that Jesus dealt with individuals on 28 occasions, whereas He preached only four sermons—a ratio of seven to one in favor of personal witnessing. If Christ put so much emphasis on individual witnessing, should we not follow His example in leading souls to Christ?

Jail Ministry

Prior to 1956, the evangelism work of Lee College was limited to one jail service in Benton, Tennessee, when students felt like going. An inmate named J.C. Todd had screamed in one of the jail services, "Blood's gonna run

41

thick when I get out of this jail." This stirred Charles' heart. Something had to be done. People like J.C. Todd lived right under the shadow of Lee College and the Church of God headquarters.

One Sunday afternoon when a group of Lee College students walked through the door of that jail, it seemed as though heaven opened in his heart. Before, J.C. Todd had just listened to the songs. When G.A. Swanson walked over to him and asked, "Do you want to become a Christian?" The sorrow J.C. had experienced for a long time came to the surface, and as he opened up his heart to the Lord, tears of sorrow gave way to tears of joy. J.C. devoured the Bible G.A. gave him. He liked the scripture "And the truth shall make you free" (John 8:32).

During the next two weeks, J.C. witnessed and testified to everyone in the jail, and three prisoners found Christ as their Savior. When he was released from jail, with the encouragement of Charles Beach, he returned to the same jail and preached the wonderful plan of salvation. One hard-crusted prisoner, who had often cursed when the students were preaching, gave his heart to the Lord. This was one of many who came to know the Lord because of J.C.'s testimony.

In 1956-57, J.B. Gaston was elected president of PFC. With the capable assistance of G.A. Swanson (who was nicknamed "Stormy"), they had four jail services a week in the county and city jails.

On one occasion when Howard Hancock gave the invitation to receive Christ, the jailer came to the bars and said, "I want to be saved." About 10 men in the jail responded to the invitation. It was a sight! The jailer on one side of the bars and the prisoners on the other side— all praying the sinner's prayer: "God, take Your precious blood and wash all my sins away. Jesus, if You'll save me, I'll live for You and I'll work for You the rest of my life."

Jail services were very important to Charles Beach. He taught the Pioneers for Christ members well. He wrote the following article in the *Encyclopedia on Evangelism*.

Conducting a Jail Service

The Lord approves of worship services in prisons and jails: "Then shall the King say . . . Come, ye blessed of my Father, inherit the kingdom prepared for you from the foundation of the world: For . . . I was in prison, and ye came unto me" (Matthew 25:34-36). Knowing that the Lord has placed His special endorsement on the efforts of those who carry His message to the unfortunate in prisons, one should pay careful attention to preservice planning.

First, obtain the permission to hold weekly services in local jails, workhouses or prisons from proper authorities, such as jailers, sheriffs or policemen. Conduct the service on a regular day on a weekly basis without interruption. Never take the jailer or person in charge of the jail for granted; ask him each week for permission to continue the service and show him proper appreciation by thanking him at the conclusion of each service for his cooperation.

Next, contact the people who will participate in the jail service. Plan a time, possibly at someone's home, for special prayer and program organization. Assign every person a function to perform during the service. Include at least two or three group songs, interspersed with personal testimonies and special songs or instrumental numbers. Give the prisoners songbooks and invite them to participate in the singing.

Beginning Service Contacts

Know that the devil, who dominates the lives of the unsaved, including the lost in prison, cannot free those whom he has imprisoned: "How art thou fallen from heaven, O Lucifer, son of the morning! . . . Is this the man . . . that made the world as a wilderness, and destroyed the cities thereof; that opened not the house of his prisoners?" (Isaiah 14:12, 17). Use your first contacts with the prisoners for whom and with whom you will conduct a worship service to establish in these men a hope in Christ, their only possible deliverer.

On entering the cell block or place prepared for the service, greet warmly the prisoners by shaking hands with as many of them as possible. Learn the names of any new inmates each week; write down the names so that you can remember to pray for them. In return, give the inmates your names and show them friendliness. This will help put them at ease for the worship service.

In your kindness, however, it is important to remember an admonition by the Reverend Troy Baggett: "Never interfere with the regular processes of law by approaching a jailer, sheriff, judge or police chief on behalf of the inmates. This is the job of the inmates' attorneys." The Christian's only task is to bring the gospel. Interference in legal matters may cancel the jail and prison services and consequently block the opportunity for these prisoners to receive the gospel.

In-Service Message

Know that Christ can deliver His own—even those in prison. "But the angel of the Lord by night opened the prison doors, and brought [the apostles] forth" (Acts 5:19).

Knowing that only the Lord can deliver those in spiritual prison, and that only the Lord has power to deliver His own from a literal prison, be certain your message of salvation and deliverance is simple and clear enough to be comprehended by those inmates who have little Bible background. End every prison message with a concise, deliberate and slow explanation of the plan of salvation: believe (Acts 16:31); confess (1 John 1:9); repent (Luke 13:3); and witness (Romans 10:9). These scriptures are dealt with more thoroughly in "How to Lead a Soul to Christ."

After the message, either the person in charge of the service or the preacher should conduct the altar call. It is confusing to the listening inmates for two or three persons to be talking to them at the same time during such an altar call.

Post-Service Counseling

Know that hope is never cut off to the living penitent. "For to him that is joined to all the living there is hope" (Ecclesiastes 9:4). As long as a man is alive and willing to repent, there is hope. You must aggressively convey this message to the inmates, because they often feel nothing but hopelessness. This should occur during the personal contact period of witnessing and counseling on an individual basis, following the conclusion of the message and altar call. Because this is the time a great many inmates in jails and prisons are won, schedule ample time at the end of the service for such counseling.

Many times those in prison tend to become bitter and filled with hate, especially toward their enemies who put them there. Therefore, during the post-service session, read Luke 6:27-35 and encourage them to love their enemies, to do good to them that hate them, and pray for them who despitefully use them. Then point out the reward

45

(in v. 35) for those who do such. Then you will have saved a soul from death and will have hidden "a multitude of sins" (James 5:20).

Street Ministry

Two regular street services were started in Cleveland in 1956. The white people heard the gospel at the Courthouse Square, and the blacks heard the gospel on Inman Street. Even though there was a great racial barrier at this time in the South, the Inman Street people received the students with open arms, because they sensed their love.

Once in the midst of a Saturday afternoon street service, a little girl who came quite often to the services had an epileptic seizure. The young man who was preaching turned and rebuked the sickness in the name of Jesus. The girl got back on her feet in a moment's time, and the sermon was continued without interruption.

Many students were given an opportunity to preach on the streets. This was the beginning for some outstanding ministers of the gospel. Gerald Johnson preached his first sermon on Inman Street. He titled his sermon, "The Great Speckled Bird," and declared, "God loves us all—red and yellow, black and white."

One day when Charles and a group of students were passing out tracts on the courthouse square, Zelma Parham approached Charles and asked him to go to her home to pray for a sick mother and father. Charles took some of the students with him and God saved an entire family and some neighbors. All of these precious converts are now in glory.

Another article written by Charles for the *Encyclopedia on Evangelism* follows.

Conducting Street and Open-Air Services

Open-air services are Biblical. Public witnessing and proclamation of the gospel have had the approval of the Lord from the beginning. Jesus started a service at a public water well and the service spread throughout the city and lasted two days; the results were that "many more believed because of his own word . . . that this is indeed the Christ, the Savior of the world" (John 4:41, 42).

Paul held an open-air service beside a river (Acts 16:13-15) and another public service on Mars' Hill in Athens before philosophers and learned men, some of whom he won to the Lord (see Acts 17:18-34).

There is no scripture that specifically commands the sinner to attend church, but there is ample scripture telling the Christian to go into the streets and public places with the gospel to persuade the sinner to come to the house of the Lord: "And the lord said unto the servant, Go out into the highways and hedges, and compel them to come in, that my house may be filled" (Luke 14:23).

The objective, therefore, of the street service is to reach the unchurched with the plan of salvation and to convince them that they need to attend church and worship God. This is evident in Christ's dealing with the woman at the well. As soon as she was convicted of her sins, she began to raise the question of the proper place to worship, in Jerusalem or on Mount Gerizim (John 4:20).

Open-air services should be well planned. Bob Blackaby gives the following instructions for effective street services:

Planning the service. It is first necessary to contact the chief of police to obtain permission to conduct a street service, designating a permanent and regular time and a permanent and regular place to hold the service. The preacher, musicians, singers and other participants must

47

be contacted early enough for them to prepare for the service. Transportation, public address systems, musical instruments, tracts and songbooks must be acquired ahead of time. The leader of the service should acquaint all the participants with the order of the services and should have prayer on behalf of the service before leaving. Upon arrival at the designated place, the leader must see to it that the equipment is set up properly, that the volume of the speaker is not blaringly loud, and that the group is formed in a semicircle around the microphone facing the audience. The leader must be sure no sidewalk or passageway is blocked by the group.

Conducting the service. The leader begins the service by announcing the church or organization the group represents, giving the address of the church and the times of the services. An invitation is extended to the listeners to attend the announced services. Next the leader announces a group song. There may be testimonies, special songs, and so forth. If prayer is offered, it should be done by one person, not by the group.

After being introduced, the preacher steps forward to the microphone and preaches a salvation message that is not offensive to other denominations and organizations. The sermon should always end with a clear explanation of the plan of salvation. After the message, which should be limited to 10 to 15 minutes, the preacher may conduct the altar call while the musicians play softly in the background.

Concluding the service. After the altar call is ended, the leader should announce that the members of the group will disperse and pass out gospel tracts. Those who are passing out tracts and witnessing to bystanders should be courteous and not argumentative. Men should deal with men, and women with women. It is extremely important to stick to the simple plan of salvation. Always get names, ages and addresses of converts for follow-up purposes.

Witnessing Teams

In the spring of 1957, Charles organized his small group of workers into a witnessing team that knocked on 100 doors. Souls found Christ. The students were encouraged to work for God. This was the beginning of something great—the beginning of a destiny.

Bill Wooten was one of the students Charles personally trained to witness using four scriptures: Acts 16:31; Luke 13:3; 1 John 1:9; and Romans 10:9. Together they led many people to the Lord. Then Charles instructed Bill to get other students to go witnessing with him. He said, "I trained you. Now you train them."

Bill's first trainee was difficult. This young man from Oklahoma would not walk on the sidewalk—he insisted on walking on the grass. Bill knew he was different, but he felt led of God to train him to be a witness. Bill went over the method of witnessing at least 15 times. Then Bill knocked on a door, witnessed to the person who answered and then went to the next house. He said to the trainee: "Now it's your turn." The young man pointed his finger at the man who answered the door and said, "Do you know you are going to hell?" The man was stunned. Then he pushed past the man at the door, went in and started preaching to the children who were watching television. Bill apologized for his partner and said, "Let me get him, and we'll get out of your hair." Then Bill raked the student over the coals just as Charles Beach would

49

have done. But it was not long until the student was witnessing effectively.

That summer Keith Black, a Spanish student, was sent to Arizona to work in the Spanish churches there. That same summer Charles and Keith attended Soul Clinic in Los Angeles, where they received the idea for the tract brigade and improvements for house-to-house witnessing. This young man blessed the lives of many in the pioneer days of the club.

Beginning of the Invasions

The school year 1957-58 brought new experiences for the club. In September 1957, Charles and some students conducted a house-to-house witnessing campaign in Ooltewah, Tennessee. The group was then renamed Pioneers for Christ. Some of the early leaders were J.B. Gaston, G.A. Swanson, Terry Beaver and Bill Wooten, who developed the idea now known as the "weekend invasion." Two churches— Ooltewah, Tennessee, and South Cleveland Church of God in Cleveland, Tennessee—invited the club to come into their churches and train their people to witness.

One of the major jobs for the students was to "route out" the area. The leaders would go out and get the names of streets for students and church members to invade. The leader would send the members of his team out two by two, a boy with a girl when possible. The leader made sure each couple had a Bible, plenty of tracts, and several 3-by-5-inch cards for addresses of new converts or church prospects. He prayed with them, assigned each couple a certain street or a certain number of blocks to cover, and sent them out to witness.

Countdown Services

In a countdown service, the pianist runs down the scale and the person in charge counts down from 10. "In 20 minutes you are going to be given an opportunity to go find some lost person and lead them to Jesus. Will you respond?" People in these first two churches where the countdown services were held were greatly challenged. Howard Hancock, a PFC member, had suggested to begin by counting down. This became a great tool in the hands of God to get people into the harvest.

G.A. Swanson wrote 50 churches offering the services of Pioneers for Christ members. Not a single answer was received. Charles and the leaders kept praying.

In January 1958, President Terry Beaver conducted the first out-of-Cleveland invasion. The invasion began in Athens, Tennessee, and continued with house-to-house witnessing in Sweetwater, Tennessee. Bill Wooten was appointed invasion leader. In October 1958, Pastor Tommy Day in Knoxville thought his church would be blessed by a surprise countdown service. He invited the group to conduct their first out-of-state invasion. During the Easter vacation 1959, a small group of students went to eastern Mississippi to Reeds Chapel, Union, Oak Ridge and Philadelphia. State Overseer Wade Horton was in every service, worshipping, praying and encouraging the young witnesses.

Child Evangelism

Children were attracted to Charles Beach. He always carried candy and gum in his pockets to give to them. Further, he communicated on their level. When he wanted to get their attention, he pulled a few magic tricks out of his pocket. This always captivated them. At that time evangelism of children was an anointing few people knew about.

Child evangelism began to expand in the college. On one occasion teacher Peggy (Humphrey) Scarborough and a group of students were witnessing to a group of children at the city dump when they spotted a woman eating out of a garbage can. They went to her and told her of Jesus Christ who could change her life. The lady asked them to go to her home and tell her family about this Jesus. They did. They went into a run-down shack and told an entire family Jesus loved them and could change their destiny. The entire family came to Christ. Wrecked lives—eating out of garbage cans—these are the people for whom Christ died.

Charles taught students how to win children to Christ. He led hundreds to Christ himself. When Charles learned about the Wordless Book, he carried one with him when witnessing to children.

The Wordless Book was easily made by gluing or stapling together five different colors of construction paper—gold (or yellow), black, red, white and green (in that order). The width and length of the book can be determined by the desire of the person using it.

He said, "Although there are no words or pictures, the book contains one of the most beautiful stories ever told." Charles used this simple story to captivate so many hearts and win many children to the Lord.

In the *Encyclopedia on Evangelism,* Charles explained the Wordless Book.

When approaching a child, use a friendly and runabout manner. For example, you might begin by saying: "Hello, sonny! What are you doing? Playing marbles? Say, you're pretty good, aren't you? Do you ever like to read books or listen to stories? You do? Can you read? Do you think that you could read a book like this? Why not? Oh, because it doesn't have any words! Well, you're right. You couldn't read it because this book has no words or pictures. But do you know what? It tells one of the most beautiful stories you've ever heard. Would you like to hear it? OK, let's sit down right here on the grass and I'll tell you all about it."

The gold (yellow) page. (Basically this is the story; of course, you will want to dress it up with your own imagination.) "You see this gold page? What can you think of that's gold? Well, your daddy's keys and your uncle's gold tooth. Have you ever seen streets? Yes, they are rather dirty and black, but did you know that in heaven there will be streets of pure gold? And this gold page stands for heaven, because in heaven the streets are paved with gold. Heaven is a glorious place where there'll be no more skinned knees or little children with crutches. It's a place where no one will ever grow old." (Continue to elaborate on what will and will not be in heaven.) "And the Bible says there will be no sin in heaven."

The black page. "And that brings us to this second page, which represents a sinful heart. Now think hard! Have you ever told Daddy a story or have you ever taken a cookie when Mommy told you not to do it? Sure, we all have done something like that; but those things are sinful in the sight of the Lord and if we want to go to heaven, something must be done about them. Jesus has provided that something."

The red page. "Do you know what red stands for? No, it's not for your little red wagon! Red, in this case, stands for the blood of Jesus. And only by the blood of Jesus can you get rid of your sins. The Bible says in 1 John 1:7, 'And the blood of Jesus Christ his Son cleanseth us from all sin.'"

The white page. "Now watch! When I take this red page and cover the black page, what color do you see? White! That's just how the blood of Jesus works. When it covers the dark and sinful heart, it becomes white and clean and pure. Would you like for your heart to be like that? Would you like to know that your sins are forgiven and that you are ready to meet Jesus if He were to come now?" (Emphasize the importance of accepting Jesus now, and then let the child know that you will pray with him at this time if he will let you. If he consents, offer to lead him in prayer).

The sinner's prayer. "Dear Jesus, I know I am a sinner, and I'm sorry for my sins. Please forgive me now as I repent and confess my sins to You. Thank You, Jesus, for hearing my prayer and saving me. Amen." (After praying with the child or children, emphasize the importance of believing from one's heart).

The green page. (Notice that the green page has not yet been used. Turn to it now.) "What can you think of that's green? Look around you. Yes, the grass is green and the trees are green. What are they doing? Yes, they are growing! And that's what this page stands for—growing in the Lord. After we accept Jesus into our hearts, we must grow in the Lord. I'm going to tell you four things that you must do in order to grow into a strong Christian. I want you to put them into practice. You must pray, read your Bible, go to church and tell other people about Jesus." (You might elaborate a little on each of these four things to do. Have the child repeat them until you are sure that he or she remembers them.)

Charles encouraged students to use this simple approach to lead children to Christ. However, it did not always go so smoothly. One day Bob Blackaby was telling some children about his Wordless Book. He fluently told them about their black hearts, the blood of Jesus and the white page representing a changed heart. He was not accustomed to using this presentation and declared, "And you'll be green the rest of your life." Some of his friends have never let him forget it.

New Convert Follow-up

Follow-up for the converts became a burden to Charles. Therefore, he developed a series of lessons that the club sent to every person won to Christ in jail services, street services, child evangelism classes or on invasions. There were special lessons even for the children. The lessons were designed to give the new convert the help to be able to stand strong and grow spiritually. There were special people whose assignment was to send out the lessons, grade them after they were sent back in and correspond with the new Christians. These lessons are included in Part 3.

The Lay Ministry's Department and the Radio Department of the Church of God used these lessons for follow-up for their converts. The Women's Ministries Department of the Church of God also used them to train Girls Club counselors. One counselor said, "I did not know how many gaps I had in my knowledge of God. It was life-changing to learn about salvation, faith, the Baptism and the second coming of Jesus." Martha Wong later said, "These lessons were perfect for training people who trained our children."

3

IGNITING A FIRE

In 1959, Charles Beach purchased his first car. Up until that time, he had ridden a bus or train wherever he went. He and Lois did not have the money prior to this time to get a car. They even walked about two miles to Cooke's to purchase their groceries. When Pioneers for Christ invasions started, he used students' cars. But in 1959 he purchased a pink Rambler so that he would have a car for Pioneers for Christ invasions. Lois seldom got to ride in the Rambler, because it was always on the road for the Lord. This car served him well until 1975 when he gave it to his nephew and bought another one. At that time it had been driven over 300,000 miles doing the work of the Lord.

The Invasion Ministry Spreads

The year 1959-60 brought new leaders to Lee College, who were destined to be great soulwinners once they came under Charles Beach's influence. Thanksgiving

1959 was a memorable time. Students were asked to go to Hamilton, Ohio, to conduct services in several churches. On this invasion, as in many to follow, Bob Blackaby became a stabilizing force and a mighty prayer warrior.

As the students drove out of Cleveland in Bob's car, they noticed a red light. Bob said, "Don't worry. Just pray." The students laid their hands on the dash of the car and asked God to keep the car and them safe and to get them to Hamilton, Ohio, and back in that car. Numerous times on the trip the red light came on. Bob called for prayer every time. The car made the trip safely, but it fell apart after the invasion.

However, this was a glorious invasion. Souls were saved, Christians blessed, and pastors encouraged. One old saint of God cried out in the service: "This is the thing on which the Church of God was born."

This same year Gerald Johnson, a dedicated Christian and soulwinner, accepted the call to preach. Aubrey Maye, the club sandwich maker, didn't realize at this time the great work God had planned for him.

Rich Ussery, one of the outstanding invasion leaders, related that it was difficult to say "No" to Charles Beach. Sometimes invasions were scheduled before exams. Rich said, "I learned that if I honored the Lord and Brother Beach, my grades would be better if I went on the invasion than if I stayed home to study." He told of an experience when he had to know 50 philosophical terms for an exam with Dr. Don Bowdle. Rich felt that he should not go on the invasion, but he could not let Brother Beach down. He went! When he came back, he set the curve on that exam. Pastor Rich Ussery testifies, "I learned that if I put God first, everything else would fall into place."

God Uses Weak Things

Charles Beach taught the students this truth: God can take the weak things of the world to confound the mighty. Ted Gee walked up to a man sitting on a porch and witnessed to him. The man acted unconcerned. Ted pointed his finger at him and said, "You're going to go to hell; and when you get there, don't say I didn't tell you so." As Ted was walking away, the man ran after him and said, "Tell me about this Jesus." The man gave his life to the Lord.

There was a student who did not dress as well as the others. He had not learned good hygiene. His breath smelled bad. It was difficult to get a witnessing partner for him. One day he walked into a house and began witnessing to a lady who was under deep conviction. The baby began to cry. The student was anxious to lead the lady and the family to the Lord. He blurted out, "Lady, put that crying young'un down, get rid of your snuff, and let me tell you about Jesus." She put the baby down and spit out her snuff. The young student led her to Jesus. Then the entire family joined in with the sinner's prayer and found Christ as Savior.

One Friday night in Roswell, Georgia, the air was charged with the power of God. Revival was in the air. Bob Blackaby stood up to preach. A student with a reputation of getting out of order began to speak in other tongues. PFC members cringed. But God was in charge of the service. An interpretation came to the message. Without an altar call being given, the altars filled with people crying and praying, surrendering their lives to Jesus Christ. The message got through loud and clear that God can take the weakest vessels and use them for His glory.

Bringing Out Potential in Students

Many students came to Lee College who had almost no self-confidence. They had no idea God had sent them into the world with sealed orders. But Charles could spot greatness in them. He had a knack for seeing special gifts in students, and they were often like sponges. Charles Beach grabbed them up, molded them and called them into service at an impressionable time in their lives.

On one occasion the East Cleveland Church of God wanted a child evangelism class. Charles asked Martha Smith Wong to take the class. That did so much for Martha's self-esteem and spiritual growth. She accepted the challenge, went door-to-door and sought out children for her class. This was the making of another great worker for the church, who later became a missionary to China and worked with girls clubs in the Women's Ministry Department of the Church of God. This was the beginning of a soul-winner who was to lead hundreds to Christ in her life-time, as well as train others to win souls. Later when Martha was in Hong Kong establishing a work for God, Lois and Charles Beach sent offerings to her every month. If God had need of it in Hong Kong, it went there. They believed their money had a mission.

Kyle Hudson, who later became a teacher in the Division of Religion at Lee University, believed Charles was instrumental in his recognition of his call to preach. Hudson said, "He put me in charge of a PFC team that was going to Oregon for the summer. He trusted me in that position, and after I got there, I found that I really could handle it. Because of that experience, I was willing to believe what I had been afraid to accept before—that God was calling me into the ministry.

Mary Margaret (Holdman) Morris writes: "In the fall of 1960, Charles Beach took a short, scared girl who had come 800 miles from home, knew no one, and who wondered if she would even make it in college, and gave me opportunities to develop spiritually." Today Mary Margaret and her husband, Jack, have ministered on five continents.

Bonding to Soulwinning Students

Charles Beach loved the soulwinning students. He went into the cafeteria every evening during the dinner hour. Going from table to table, he talked with those who had been out witnessing that day, asking about their experiences and telling them about his own encounters. Encouragement for soulwinning was a daily routine.

One of the most encouraging experiences that launched PFC forward was an invasion in Dillon, South Carolina. Fifty students were invited to the state prayer conference that was meeting in Dillon. Pastors and their wives, as well as laypeople, went witnessing with the students. That one afternoon 105 souls were gloriously saved. Many of them came to the service that night. Revival fires burned!

Invasions Brought Revival

The invasions became a great blessing to the churches. Pastors stopped seeing the teams merely as opportunities to give students a chance to preach. The students began winning souls and bringing them into the churches. They were igniting church growth. When the students left, the churches were never the same.

One such incident happened in Flint, Michigan. Glenna Sheppard (Lee) was witnessing with Jim Forester, the son of the pastor of the West Flint Church of God. It was a rainy day, and Glenna was concerned that she might scare the people in the houses. They knocked on a door. A lady with four children came to the door. Glenna said, "We are not trying to talk you into coming to our church, but we just want to ask you if you know Jesus." The lady responded, "No, but I would like to." Jim held the baby while Glenna led this precious lady to the Lord. Years later Pastor T.L. Forester told Glenna that the woman came to church and brought her entire family. They became stable members of the church.

In Lucedale, Mississippi, Wanda Blackaby (Fox), one of the lady preachers on the team, was praying, "Oh God! Why can't we see a mighty move of Your Spirit?" Suddenly the Holy Ghost was manifest in that church as the students had never seen in their lives. This was a life-changing experience. Souls were saved, bodies were healed.

Discipline Learned on Invasions

Charles had a strong sense that students should be responsible leaders on these invasions. His philosophy was this: "If you sleep on it, make it up. If you wear it, hang it up. If you drop it, pick it up. If you eat out of it, wash it. If you step on it, wipe it up. If it rings, answer it. If it howls, feed it." He wanted the students to be disciplined followers of the Lord. He believed that God made servants, and servants became leaders. Charles transferred his spirit of servanthood to many students. He believed that the heart of a true leader is servanthood. He realized that the anointing was for those who were willing to pay the price. His students always left a great reputation and testimony behind them.

Pioneers for Christ members saw the great desire Charles Beach had to please the Lord. Thus, they developed a passion to please him. Sometimes it was tough on young college students, but in the end, leaders were born.

Doug LeRoy was a new invasion leader. His assignment was to take a team to Shelby, North Carolina. They met at 4 a.m. for breakfast. On the way, one of the cars had an accident. Charles stayed behind with the problem, and Doug took the other students on to Shelby.

When Charles arrived, he went to the home where two of the men were staying. They had not made up their beds. The lady of the house had told them not to make the beds because she wanted to change the sheets. Brother Beach told the guys, "We make up beds on invasions." Then he personally went in and made up the beds. The lady came right behind him and pulled the sheets off to wash them.

Then Doug became more frustrated. He made the mistake of asking Charles if he wanted to teach a Sunday school class. The answer was, "No! The Pioneers for Christ members do the teaching!"

Arriving back on campus, Doug and Charles met to review the trip. "Doug, you've got it in you to be a great leader, but you've got to get those under you under subjection. You have to show them what to do." Doug was a dynamic speaker and leader, but he became frustrated. He went into the dorm and spoke to Aubrey Maye and John Lombard. "I can evangelize. I don't need Charles Beach," he said. Aubrey and John shared their experiences with him. "But, Doug," they said, "He is making leaders out of us. We need it. Hang in there with us." Doug LeRoy decided to get on board and be submissive to the authority of those God had placed in his life. He knew that if he were under authority, he would have authority. And he longed to have authority to bring deliverance to the captives. What a powerful leader he has become for the Church of God and the kingdom of God. Having Charles Beach as a mentor shaped his entire destiny to be a leader of excellence for God's work.

One morning a PFC president overslept and missed a meeting. "Did you eat breakfast today?" asked Charles. "Yes," the student replied. "Did you eat lunch?" "Yes." "Did you eat dinner?" "Yes." "That is your problem. Your stomach is your god." Mr. Beach believed you had to have radical training for radical warriors.

Mitch Maloney and a group of students had been sent to Ohio to minister with a group not connected with Pioneers for Christ. One of the girls had worn a short skirt. Someone contacted Dr. James Cross, who was president of Lee College at that time. Mitch was in the rest room in the Alumni Building when he met Charles. "Are you Mitch Maloney?" he asked. "I am." "Well, you took an invasion team into Ohio, and a girl wore a skirt entirely too short. Now we may never be able to get Pioneers for Christ back into Ohio!"

This was Mitch's introduction to the great man of God. He didn't like the whole scene. He then went into the chapel service. As he worshiped, God convicted his heart. Afterward, he went looking for Charles and apologized. Once Charles saw Mitch's commitment, they became close friends. Mitch now describes their relationship by referring to an illustration by Joel Osteen when he assumed his father's pulpit. Joel said, "I inherited my daddy's car. I can drive it. I have my daddy's tie. I can wear it. I have on my daddy's suit. I can wear it, but I had to cut it down to my size." Mitch often says, "That's the way I feel about Charles Beach."

Dangerous for a Sinner to Walk on Campus

Students became so excited about soulwinning it became dangerous for a sinner to walk on the campus. One unsaved person came on campus and was witnessed to by six students. When Doug LeRoy became president of PFC, it was estimated that 70 percent of the campus was involved in outreach ministry. When the club first started, Bill Wooten had prophesied, "The day will come when it will be unpopular not to be a member of the Pioneers for Christ." That day came. The campus became an army! Charles Beach beamed, because he knew this was the thing for which he had been born. He said, "It has become evident that personal soulwinning is not a passing emotional whim of unstable youths, but it is a burning passion." He was proud of this group of students.

Christian Service Director

Charles Beach was soon appointed Christian service director of the college. It was as Mordecai said to Esther, "Who knoweth whether thou art come to the kingdom for such a time as this" (Esther 4:14). This was the crucial moment that launched Charles into one of the greatest soulwinning ministries in the body of Christ in the 20th century.

Charles wrote an article in the *Evangel* titled "Lee Bible College—From Classroom Theory to Field Application."

In this article he explained the philosophy of Lee Bible College concerning soulwinning. He maintained that the primary purpose of the Bible College was the preparation of young men and women for the ministry in the Church of God. He believed that there must be a marriage of the theoretical and the practical in order to thoroughly train young leaders. He felt that the Bible College was strong under the leadership of men like Dean Hollis Gause, and it became his principle ministry to provide students with ample opportunities to apply the know-how they received in the classroom. In this article he wrote his philosophy of the Pioneers for Christ.

Witnessing. The student is first taught how to witness and win souls through personal evangelism. Charles often reminded students to get their converts witnessing. He told them about the Samaritan woman at the well, who went immediately after having accepted Christ and witnessed to others in the city. "And many . . . of that city believed on him for the saying of the woman, which testified" (John 4:39).

Cooperation. The student's next step was to learn to work with others in order to realize more fully the value of cooperation. As an example, many of the new students' earlier witnessing attempts were with other, more experienced students. They learned the art of cooperation by teaching someone else how to win the lost to Christ.

Planning. After the students learned how to witness and appreciated the value of cooperation, they were permitted to go behind the scenes and help in the planning of witnessing invasions and various other services. Charles felt that this aspect of training would be valuable to the students in other endeavors of ministry.

Responsibility. The next training process was accepting responsibilities and carrying them out. Within every group there were responsibilities of leading, planning, singing, directing, teaching, preaching and witnessing. Students who performed their responsibilities well were then assigned to the leadership of a group. In this position, many of their previous experiences in witnessing, cooperation, planning an invasion and other responsibilities were brought back into play each time they led a group in a service or activity.

Students Covered the Nation

There was no city or town too small or too large for Pioneers for Christ. Students were sent by Charles Beach all over the nation. They went in old cars and new cars, to large and small churches. But God used them everywhere they went. They were self-sacrificing. They had caught the spirit of their mentor.

Bob Blackaby was on one of the invasions in Fort Worth, Texas. He and the parents of Billy O'Neal went out witnessing together. They led a couple to the Lord, both of whom were in their 80s. That same week the newly converted couple (both of them) went home to be with the Lord—saved in the very last minutes of their lives.

Foreign Study

Charles had a great desire for excellence. Even though he had great training in foreign languages, he spent several summers studying in foreign countries. His additional studies were at the Université de Paris (Sorbonne), Alliance Française (Paris), Institut de Phonétique (Paris) and Goethe Institut (Germany). He became known as a great teacher.

Determination to See the Army Successful

With a heavy teaching load, some wondered how Charles could spend so much time witnessing and training students to witness. Charles responded, "I am going to see that God's work gets done if it harelips the devil." His daughter, Sharlinda, wrote, "Most of Dad's waking, and what should have been sleeping hours were spent in prayer, research and study, writing, and planning and discussing his goal of winning the lost. He knew he would have been lost had someone not shared the gospel with him, and he did not want to lose any time in sharing the gospel with as many others as possible."

4

SUMMER WITNESSING TEAMS

In the summer of 1960, Lee College students began to devote their entire summers to the work of God. Martha Smith Wong and Mary Brannon Betancourt went to the Bahamas. Charles Beach and Bill Wooten went to Knoxville to teach the church members to become effective witnesses for Christ.

Charles often prayed for God to give him leaders who would help him propel this church forward in soul-winning. In September 1960, Cecil B. Knight became national Sunday school and youth director, with Don Aultman as his assistant. Ray H. Hughes became president of Lee College. These three men became a tremendous backbone for the Pioneers for Christ work. They met with Charles and said, "If Mormons can send out their elders, we can send out dedicated witnesses into the harvest field of the Lord." Under the sponsorship of the National Sunday School and Youth Department, Pioneers for Christ sent Martha Smith Wong and Karen Lily Conine to the Bahamas during the following summer.

In the summer of 1961, Charles, in cooperation with the National Sunday School and Youth Department, initiated the first summer witnessing program to work with teenage drug addicts in Providence, Rhode Island, and New York City.

Students Building a Church in Rhode Island

After finishing his last class that spring day in 1961, Ray Sanders was walking across the Lee College campus to the campus barbershop, which he operated, when Brother Beach approached him. "Ray, how would you like to go on one of the first summer witnessing teams to Providence, Rhode Island?" Ray quickly responded, "Brother Beach, I would like to, but it was announced in chapel this morning that all school bills must be paid if we wanted to return to Lee next year. Plus, I have to work this summer to pay for my car." The response was quick: "OK, just let people die and go to hell while you pay for that piece of metal and get your education."

Charles walked away, smacking his gums and rubbing his forehead. Ray walked on to the barbershop in the basement of Walker Hall, but the words kept ringing in his ears, "Let people die and go to hell while you pay for that piece of metal." Ray could stand it no longer. He opened the door, put his books on the shelf and dashed out the door, running across the campus looking for Charles. When he found him, Ray told him if he would let him go, he was ready. Ray didn't find out until later that a team had already been selected, but no one on the team had a car. Those words transformed Ray Sanders' life. He was never the same.

That summer Ray Sanders, Gerald Johnson, Dickey Davis, Sue McGee, Betty Robbins, Martha Short and David Barnes went to Providence, Rhode Island—a Catholic-dominated city—to build a Church of God in three-months, time. Humanly speaking, this seemed like an impossible job.

They found a place to worship in the Meatcutters Hall at 824 Westminster Avenue. They never knew which room they could use or which floor it would be on. The students knocked on doors every day and invited people to the Meatcutters Hall, but they could not tell them on which floor they would be worshiping.

It was a very rough area. Someone said that it was the most wicked place they had ever seen. But the students preached every night and witnessed every day. People began to come and were saved. Zella Alacosky was their first convert. Then the Gilereth family came. Soon many others followed. A church was being birthed. Sometimes the students preached to themselves and then headed for the streets to preach at night. They preached and prayed until things happened.

One man came to the meetings and offered to give some of the people a ride home. They later found out he was taking them by his church and baptizing them in Jesus' name.

Gerald Johnson led a young man named Dewayne to the Lord. His father, Clyde, made fun of the team. He was ashamed of them. But God began to give the students favor. This man gambled on horses. He would slip money to Ray and say, "I want to give this to you if you'll take it." Ray had a quick answer: "The devil has had it long enough." Soon the entire family was converted.

71

Somebody paid Ray's car payment every month. He always believed it was Charles Beach. When the summer was over, Dr. Ray Hughes, president of Lee College, called to see when they were leaving to come home. Ray said, "I'm not going home. We have knocked on doors and preached every night. Somebody has to stay here and get this church established." Dr. Hughes said, "I'll have a replacement for you by Christmas." But Christmas came, and Ray could not leave. It took 15 months to get the church on a solid foundation.

One night he preached to himself. He even went to the altar after he gave the altar invitation. Then he heard footsteps. A man had brought in two large bags of groceries. He prophesied in his broken English: "My dear brudder, God has sent you to this city. I have listened to the entire service. You just thought you were alone." This man became a friend to Ray Sanders and together they won many people to the Lord. Many times Charles Beach sent personal offerings. At other times, he sent money he had received in chapel at Lee. Every month somebody paid Ray's car payment—probably Charles Beach.

Ray's 15 months of labor paid off. Today there is a Church of God in that city as a monument to what God can do when young people dare to trust Him. When Ray came back to school, his tuition was paid—again, probably paid by Charles Beach.

Ray Sanders and the others on that summer team learned leadership that has followed them throughout their ministries. Charles Beach taught them to invest in people and work hard. While Ray was overseer of Eastern North Carolina, I spoke for a ladies retreat led by Kathy Sanders. One night Ray was mopping the kitchen floor as he did after each evening service. I said, "Overseers don't have to mop the floor." Ray's response was, "I learned this from Charles Beach."

Five churches have since been birthed out of that Providence, Rhode Island, church. What a tribute to Charles Beach and the Pioneers for Christ members who paved the way for this great work!

Working With Dave Wilkerson's Ministry

Under the direction of Charles Beach, college teacher Peggy Humphrey, Aubrey Maye, Esdras Betancourt and Mary Margaret Holdman went to New York City to work with Dave Wilkerson in Teen Challenge. What a summer!

When they arrived in the city, it was getting dark. They saw people lying in the streets. The Holy Spirit spoke to them and said, "These are the people for whom Christ died." They knew they were on a mission.

When they arrived at the center in Brooklyn, they were excited. However, that night Dave called them all together and said, "We're going into the streets. Be prepared for anything. Last year one of my workers was beaten with chains." He then prayed, "Lord, if You have to take anybody, take me. Don't take my workers." Although these young workers were frightened, their fear soon disappeared when they saw 15-year-old boys and girls hooked on drugs.

One night a rough-looking Spanish girl came to the meeting. While Dave preached, tears streamed down her face. Milta was a war counselor for the Bishop Gang. She led the gang when they went against rival gangs. She brought up the rear when the police were after them. She explained that the ugly scar across her face came from a gang fight. That night she was gloriously saved. However, the next night Milta came to the female workers, "I can't go home," she said. "The police are there. When I got saved, gang members went to my mother and told her everything I had previously done." The young college workers went home with Milta. They convinced the police and Milta's mother to let her go to the center and stay with them for a few days. They all agreed. She became a powerful witness.

Many nights workers would get up during the night. They often noticed Milta's bed was empty. They would find her in the chapel with her face buried in the carpet, praying for hours. She would give her testimony on the street before rival gang members. "A few months ago I would not come into your territory without my gang with me. I have no gang with me tonight but the Jesus gang, and they won't hurt you. Tonight I am here to tell you how Jesus changed my life, and how He can change yours too." Many like her found Jesus to be Lord of their lives.

Once she got away from the group in a park. When they found her, she was witnessing to a policeman. With tears streaming down his face, this former gang girl told him of the love of Jesus.

Lucky was another person who came to Christ in one of those street meetings. The courts had said he was incorrigible. On one occasion, he tried to stomp his teacher's eyes out with the cleats in his shoes, but Jesus changed his life.

Two young brothers were on their way to a rumble when they passed the street meeting. They stopped and listened. The Holy Spirit convicted their hearts, and they were saved. They testified later that they were on their way to murder another teenage boy that very night.

There were other miracles that summer. Mary Margaret Holdman and I were on a street that seemed to be vacated. Suddenly a lady appeared with bandages all over her body. We stopped her and told her of the love of Jesus to heal. The lady was completely healed.

Teams Sent to the Regions Beyond

In the summer of 1962, students were sent to Jamaica, Barbados, Trinidad, the Bahamas, Salt Lake City, Boston, Albuquerque and New York City.

Thousands came to Christ in Jamaica, Barbados and Trinidad. Don Aultman went with the Pioneers for Christ to these three Caribbean islands. The students witnessed to many who worshiped all kinds of gods. But these people found the real God, who was the miracle-worker. In this group, there was a student named Teresa Peters from Mattawamkeag, Maine. There is more about her witnessing in the next chapter. In later years, Doug LeRoy met people in England who had been won to Christ on that invasion.

Panama became a targeted area for Pioneers for Christ. Students went far into the jungles to conduct services and to witness. On one occasion John Lombard, Rena Howell, Jeannie Jones, Betty Robbins and others rode horseback for 16 hours to get to the church meeting. After riding all night, they arrived about 3 a.m. One of the biggest problems was that they were one horse short, so the students took turns walking. It was a miracle of God that they survived without being bitten by the dangerous snakes in that area.

For one of the meetings way back in the jungle, they borrowed one of the pastor's car. They had 33 flat tires in 30 days. The people brought torches to light the church.

The Beginning of the Invasion of the Mormons

Bob Blackaby, under the direction of Charles Beach, led the first team of 12 to the Mormon headquarters in Salt Lake City. Mormon elders said, "We'll put a temple in Cleveland." Spirit-filled youth said, "We'll put a Church of God in Salt Lake City." The Mormons have never put a temple in Cleveland, but young people established a Church of God in Salt Lake City.

Trying to begin a church in Salt Lake City was very difficult. One night they had conducted service, not expecting too much. A little girl came to the altar and said, "I want the Lord to hide my sins." This was the beginning! They then conducted a Vacation Bible School with 55 children in attendance, right there in Mormon headquarters.

Charles loved the work in Salt Lake City. Until his death, he continued to return there to witness. On one trip, he felt compelled by the Holy Spirit to stop in three cities and knock on every door, telling people the plan of salvation. As hard as it was, he led many to Jesus Christ. But when Charles told about that experience, he admitted that he almost became a chicken and did not obey the Lord. He said, "I knocked on every door with fear and trembling." When he drove through Provo, Utah, he saw the jail. The Enemy said, "See there. They will put you in that jail." Realizing the source of the voice, he turned around and began knocking on doors. He said, "Devil, you won't stop me." Before he left that city, he knocked on 22,000 doors. He slept on an air mattress in the back of his Rambler station wagon at night and witnessed all day for days without any rest. Charles Beach never spared himself. Soulwinning was serious business with him.

On one occasion Charles and Bob Blackaby were driving out to Salt Lake City. Bob was one of the very few people Charles allowed to drive his car. Charles had fallen asleep. Tired from driving great distances around narrow roads with boulders on each side, Bob pulled off the road and dozed off to sleep. When he woke up, he thought he was still driving. Bob yelled, "I got it!" Charles shouted, "No, I got it!" Bob yelled again and Charles yelled again. Then suddenly they both woke up and realized they were sitting in a parked car fighting over the steering wheel. Moments like this have created entertaining conversations for years.

Winning the Lost on His Way

Often Charles would get in his pink Rambler and drive to Salt Lake City alone. But he did not wait until he got there to witness. He witnessed all along the way. On one occasion he and Bob Blackaby were going through Arizona on their way to Salt Lake City, when suddenly they came upon a serious wreck. A tractor-trailer had turned over. The people had already been pulled out and laid down on the road. Charles grabbed his big Bible and got down beside them on the road. He told them the plan of salvation and led them to the Lord right there. Two more souls entered the kingdom of heaven.

He transferred his church membership in Ogden, Utah, so he could pay his tithes there regularly. This church was always another home church to him.

He not only trained those who went to Salt Lake City to witness to Mormons, but he also trained all the PFC members in witnessing to the cults. One day a group of Mormons showed up on campus. Betty Robbins rushed into his classroom and said, "They are here." Charles responded, "Too bad. I've got a class to teach! You take care of them."

Boston, Massachussetts

Boston, Massachusetts, was another tough city, but Charles kept encouraging the students. The first summer they went there, the Boston strangler was on the loose. People were afraid to answer their doors. Students knocked on door after door with no results. It was discouraging. But Charles never failed to call and lift them up.

Finally, they got a breakthrough when they started holding street meetings. One night Ray Sanders was there with them. When he began to preach on the street corner, a lady came at him yelling. She was so drunk she did not know what she was saying. I went to her, got her away from Ray, sat down on a bench and began to talk with her. I was getting nowhere with her, so I kissed the lady on the cheek and said, "Jesus loves you and so do I." It was as if the lady sobered immediately. She wept, "Nobody has ever kissed me." The lady was saved that very night.

The beginning of the church came when one lady found a tract in a laundromat. A student had given someone a tract. They had laid it down, but God's Word did not go out in vain. A lady found the tract and brought her entire family to church. They invited others who began coming to the services.

Knocking on Thousands of Doors All Over the Nation

One summer Bob Blackaby and John Simms knocked on over 6,000 doors in the state of Ohio. Others did the same thing in other states.

Each year the number of homes covered by PFC doubled. In 1963-64, the group visited 84,000 homes. In 1962 they took all the ministers who attended the General Assembly with them as they witnessed. There was always an average of 50,000 homes visited.

It was not always easy for the students or Charles Beach. On one occasion a man pulled a knife on Betty Robbins right on the street. But Charles taught these young people the power of prayer.

One student knocked on a man's door and walked into a beer party that had been going on for two days. Another was told that if he didn't leave the man's property immediately, he would call the police. One woman picked a student up and threw him off her porch. One man chased a student out of his yard with a cane. But nothing stopped this mighty army.

Sponsored Many Teams Personally

Charles Beach personally sponsored many of the invasions and summer trips. He cared so much that over the years he put over $25,000 of his own money into the club. He personally drove at his own expense to be with almost every summer witnessing team. At the end of the summer, he took the students all out to a wonderful restaurant to show them his appreciation.

He Never Let You Quit

Dan Boling enrolled at Lee College, excited about being a witness for Christ. But, as most students did then, he had to work. Brother Beach approached him before the summer teams went out. "Dan, how do you feel about taking a team to Chicago to work with Ray Sanders this summer?"

"Brother Beach, I would love to," Dan replied. "But nobody is paying my way through school, and I have to work." Brother Beach turned and quickly responded: "OK. Let all those people go to hell." Then he walked away.

Dan was crushed. He went to his room and prayed all night. The next morning he asked Charles, "Who is on the team going to Chicago?" "You have to recruit them," Charles replied. "How are we going to get the finance?" asked Dan. "You have to raise it." "So how much is it going to cost?" Dan persisted. "That's your job to calculate it," was Charles' answer. Dan was new to all this, but he counted the cost and went to Chicago with a team of students he recruited.

It was a great summer. Students worked hard. People were saved, healed and delivered. But one day Dan's '56 Chevy stopped running. He would put it in drive, and it would hum. He would put it in reverse, and it would hum. They needed this car.

Members of the team went to lunch with a pastor from Indianapolis. Dan decided not to go along. He wasn't hungry because of all of the attacks he was facing from the Enemy. He decided it was time for an encounter with God. He went into the church, got the bottle of anointing oil, went outside and poured oil all over the hood of that station wagon. Immediately, he got into his car and put it into drive. It was healed! They drove that wagon the rest of the summer.

Two days before time to go back to school, the team had a major attack. Dan got up that morning and found that someone had stripped his car. It was not worth trying to fix, so he found someone to buy what was left of it. That gave him enough money to fly the students home. He called Charles to tell him they were going to rest the last two days before they flew home. His car had been stripped, and they were in a very rough area. The students were tired and needed a break before beginning school again. Charles got quiet. Then he blurted out, "But you have two more days. Souls are going to hell. You can't quit! Don't quit!" Dan replied, "But we don't have a car." Beach answered, "Leave that to me. Just keep working! If you're in a bad neighborhood, the people need to find the Lord. Don't quit!"

Shortly Cecil Knight, the state overseer of Indiana, called and said, "Dan, I am sending my Buick down for you to use these last two days." It was as if the spirit of Charles Beach had fallen on Cecil Knight. So Dan and the students continued to work those last two days before returning to school.

When Dan walked into the accounting office at Lee College to explain that his bill was not paid because he had been on a summer invasion, he received another surprise. One of the bookkeepers asked, "What are you talking about? Your school bill is paid in full." Dan always thought it was Charles, but the only thing Charles would say was, "God always takes care of those things." When Dan pushed him for an answer, Charles replied, "Do you think I would do that?" The experiences Dan had with Charles Beach changed his life forever.

When Dr. Cecil Knight called Dan Boling about going to Montana as state overseer, he remembered the summer invasion. "Dan, do you remember Chicago summer witnessing team?" he asked. "Well, you're gonna have to work just that hard in Montana."

Education of Students Was Important

Students were of great importance to him. Erlene Burton had gone on a summer witnessing team to New England. Because she was unable to work that summer, it appeared that she would not be able to return to school the following year. One of the PFC leaders told Charles that Erlene would not be back. He sent this message: "You will be back in school if you have to live at our house." She was one of many students who were encouraged by this great man of God and his precious wife, Lois.

He personally paid for another young girl named Trudy to spend an entire year studying in France. Many students have testified that Charles Beach personally paid their school bills.

He did such things as send a missionary's wife money to buy a new dress. On one occasion, he helped an impoverished boy get the money to purchase books that helped him go on to become a doctor.

Relationships With Students

Charles established a warm relationship with students. Dr. Paul Conn, who is now president of Lee University, said, "Mr. Beach is the perfect language teacher. He loves his subject, and students can sense that enthusiasm." Dr. Conn recalls the time that Charles went out of his way to give him a ride to Little Rock, Arkansas. Because Paul was in Charles' Spanish class, they decided to practice speaking nothing but Spanish for 60 miles or so at a time. Dr. Conn said, "I must have felt very much at ease with him as a freshman to ask him for a ride and to be willing to try my Spanish out on my teacher."

One of the foreign students was with him on a long trip. When Charles became sleepy, he suggested, "Let's stop and get a cup of coffee." The student said, "I don't drink coffee. I'm sanctified." Charles said, "You don't think I am sanctified?" They got into a long heated debate. The student related the story of the coffee/sanctification dispute on campus. Someone asked, "What happened?" He answered, "I had two cups of coffee."

Twice the student body at Lee College elected Charles "Teacher of the Year," and his colleagues honored him with the Excellence in Teaching Award in 1974.

Excellence in the Classroom

Charles knew how to bring the best out of students, because he saw potential others did not see. When he came across strong to them, it was because he wanted to develop discipline in them so they would be all God wanted them to be.

When Bryan Cutshall, now one of the outstanding pastors in the denomination, took English from Charles, he turned in what he thought was an excellent paper. When he got the paper back, there was a big "C" on the top. He confronted his teacher. Dr. Beach became angry. He uttered these words: "Bryan, you have a book inside you and you don't even know it. God has a plan for you to write, but you will never do it writing junk like this. Do it again." Bryan was stunned. But God had started speaking to him through his mentor. He wrote it over with great care and received an "A." Those words proved prophetic. At the time of this writing, Bryan Cutshall has published five best-seller books, 14 training manuals and several magazine articles. There are other writings waiting to be birthed. Dr. Cutshall, pastor of a great church in St. Louis, writes: "I am glad he saw in me something I could not see in myself." On one occasion he wrote Charles a letter thanking him for the "C" and the straight talk.

Dan Boling got a "C" on a test. Charles fussed, "You ought to have more pride in yourself than that. You're from Texas." Dan Boling gives much credit to Charles Beach for developing discipline in his life.

Charles tried desperately to help students learn. He once said, "A person's basic intelligence doesn't impress me. What I care about is how hard a person is willing to work and how much it means to him to know something." He told his students, "Knowledge is a wonderful thing. It doesn't matter whether you can do anything with a piece of information or not. What matters is just knowing it. Learning is a gift. It's priceless."

He made learning fun. One student had a noticeable North Carolina drawl. It was the highlight of Mr. Beach's day to get this North Carolina student to speak French.

5

TEACHER OF TEACHERS

C harles was head of the Language Department
and a great blessing to other teachers. Carolyn
Dirksen, one of the teachers in Charles' department, is now a vice president of Lee University. She
described him as a "teacher of teachers."

I hear the sharp staccato of his footsteps on the stair-
way to my office, and I sit back and wait for the surprise. Which Charles Beach will appear in my door-
way, brimming with enthusiasm and always in a
hurry? Will it be Charles Beach, the department
chairman, rushing in with a schedule to be reviewed,
very professional and efficient? It may be Charles
Beach, the scholar, bursting in with immeasurable
excitement to share his latest idea about the English
verb system. Or will it be Charles Beach, the lay witness, dropping by to relate an experience he had
while visiting in the hospital?

Whichever is to appear, I wait eagerly; for each one
is a welcome guest. The door pops open, and it is

Charles Beach, the comedian. "I know teachers in my department are underpaid, so here's your semester bonus." With a twinkle in his eye and looking very much like Charley Weaver, he scatters a handful of bubble gum on my desk. "Pretty girls from Arizona always like bubble gum." He disappears as quickly as he came, having brightened my day as he so often does by taking time for me in the rush of his demanding responsibilities.

Charles fills many roles in one day: teacher, department chairman, executive secretary of the Department of Lay Affairs, and lay evangelist at the North Cleveland Church of God witnessing to hundreds of families on Cleveland's impoverished east side. To each of these roles, Charles brings a warmth and enthusiasm that make him a most memorable and influential person.

Charles' quick wit and easy-going temperament are not a mask for an undisciplined mind. He demands much of himself and expects much of others—a quality that brings out the dedication and best efforts of those who surround him. However, in spite of his demand for professionalism from his students and coworkers, Charles never seems formidable. His rumpled suit jacket bulges with candy, which he freely gives to needy children, Lee students and fellow faculty members alike. His sparkling eyes, Charley Weaver's sense of humor and friendly manner instantly puts all the teachers at ease, and this first impression of amiability is justified by his consistent concern for those around him.

Because of being so respected, he was given an honorary doctorate from Lee College in 1984. He served 34 years as a professor of English, French, German, Spanish and personal evangelism. He was also the chairman of the

Language Department. He retired from Lee College in 1988 with the honorable title, "Professor Emeritus of Romance Languages." His honors at Lee College were many: He was awarded the Church of God Distinguished Educator Award in 1976 and was recognized by his alma mater—Lee University—with the 1964 Distinguished Alumnus of the Year Award.

Strong, Bold, Caring, Yet Human

Charles Beach was sensitive, compassionate and caring. He was a true perfectionist—full of energy and hyperactivity. Sometimes he had to deal with his temper. He would give you his last penny, but don't misuse an offering that came in for God's work.

One of Charles' greatest callings was to mentor people in the work of God. Sometimes God used him to "get the flies out of the ointment." Sometimes God used him to zero in on things that were wrong, either on invasions or in a student's life. But people who really had a heart for soulwinning realized that in order to be adequately trained by their mentor, they had to submit to him as unto the Lord. Sometimes it was pleasant to submit, sometimes it was difficult.

One student said, "If you have never been told off by Charles Beach, you have never been told off." This was because of his military background. One small error could have meant death to his comrades. He carried that same concern into the work of God. One error could mean the eternal destiny of souls. Also, he fasted lunch every day. Sometimes his potassium became low, causing deep feelings about issues that already concerned him.

Charles was sincere about everything he did. On one occasion he asked Cecil Knight to come to the Fellowship Hall and speak to the students about the harvest. When Dr. Knight finished, tears were flowing down Charles' face. He said, "I brought Brother Knight over here to shape you students up. All he did was preach me under conviction. I guess I'll just have to quit worrying about you and pray for you."

He Influenced Students by His Personal Witnessing

Bryan Cutshall was a member of Pioneers for Christ who conducted a service every Thursday in the Bradley County Nursing Home. He watched Charles go from room to room visiting patients, encouraging them, leading them to Christ. Dr. Cutshall says: "The imprint of that scene is embedded in my soul."

Charles' influence extended throughout his life. Mark Schrade, who is now an outstanding pastor, was a student at Lee in 1979. He writes: "I began to visit the hospitals with Mr. Beach regularly. He skillfully explained the gospel to each person, handling any objections with expert Biblical knowledge and boyish charm until he led them to the moment he had been longing for—their acceptance of Jesus Christ as their Lord and Savior. His joy when others were saved was often greater than the new converts' response themselves. I can remember his compassion, joy and sincerity coming through as he walked to the next room with moist eyes, thanking God for another person who had come to Christ. It was not uncommon for Charles to lead five or more people to the Lord each night."

He Influenced Graduates in Their Witnessing After Graduation

Phil and Yaunna Higgins are other examples of students Charles influenced while they were at Lee College and later while they were carrying the gospel to the lost of the world. They attended Lee during the years 1967-71. Phil was a PFC officer and learned much about leadership and evangelism from Charles.

Phil was appointed as a metropolitan evangelist in 1971. His assignment was church planting for the Church of God. During 1971-72, he went to Denver, Colorado, to work with Ray Sanders. Together they planted a church in Boulder, Colorado. Then Phil and Yaunna were sent to New York City. Here they planted about 58 churches in that needy harvest field during the years 1972-75 and then back again in 1976-80. In 1975-76, the Executive Committee sent him to Oklahoma City to plant a new church, then back to New York.

Those were exciting days. Phil worked closely with Overseer J.D. Golden and hundreds came to Christ. He worked with the ethnic leaders, training them and planting churches. One of the churches they planted averaged about 300 people; another averaged 350. Then in 1980 Phil and Yaunna were sent to San Francisco.

During these times, Charles was very close to Phil and Yaunna. They would talk on the phone for hours. When Phil encountered difficulty, especially with the cults, he would call his former PFC director. Together they would strategize on the phone how to win the cultists to Christ. Charles gave such sound advice on what topics to deal with and what to stay away from. He advised Phil to meet the leadership with the prospect present. Because of Charles' wise counsel, Phil was able to win many cultists to Christ. Charles often said, "The Scriptures will work in any situation."

Phil and Yaunna worked diligently in the harvest field. They kept PFC teams and pastors and their wives in their home. Yaunna was an anointed soloist for every imaginable cultural group. She directed the women's ministry and organized children's ministries until she physically dropped from exhaustion. She needed to be hospitalized. But instead, Phil lay by her side reading from the Word of God for hours. He had been so greatly influenced by Charles Beach to believe that the Word works! He read the Word until Yaunna was able to read it for herself again. Soon she was completely healed. That experience reiterated the truth in them: If you have the Word of God, you don't have to have anything else.

Charles Beach Held Back Nothing

That pink Rambler that Charles totally gave to the work of the Lord had over 300,000 miles on it when he gave it to his nephew. He transferred so much to his followers. A number of students had done exactly what their mentor had done—given their vehicle to God's work.

Ray Sanders put over 142,000 miles on his car while he was a student. Ray said, "I might have been in Alabama, but my car may have been in Mexico."

Howard Hancock recalls burning up two cars for PFC. He had a '40 Ford. On one invasion in Mississippi, there was not enough room in the trunk for all the luggage. Girls always took extra luggage, so they put the suitcases on top of the car. The luggage was so heavy the entire top of the car caved in. Finally, Howard bought a '50 Ford. They took this car to Monterrey, Mexico. When the car began burning oil, it looked as though it was on fire going down the highway. Smoke was coming up through the floor of the car. Aubrey Maye and Howard took handkerchiefs and placed over their mouths. They looked like bandits.

That generation, like their mentor, gave everything they had to work for the Master. Today many of these people still have that spirit of giving everything to God.

Working on Lee College Accreditation

During the years when Lee College was working on accreditation, Charles and Lois Beach were key players. Charles was sent to other colleges to get ideas on what was needed to make Lee College a better school. Don Aultman, vice president of the college at that time, said, "Charles was significant because of the great influence he and Lois had on the faculty. Further, he wrote many of the materials that were needed for the association." During this time, the faculty was being called upon to make many adjustments. Charles Beach helped teachers and administrators through that transition. He worked as diligently for the accreditation of the school as he did for Pioneers for Christ. It was God's school and he wanted the best possible education and opportunities for the students.

Taught Students to Be Mentors of Others

Mentoring involves the leader pouring his life into his protégé. Many things are caught, rather than taught. Charles Beach poured his life into his students. Then they poured their lives into others.

Ray Sanders and Randy Hamon were examples. Randy led a group to Minnesota in 1975. On that team were Barbara Fleming, Maracia Ray, Floria Brown, Charlotte Willis, David Smart and Tom Batchelor. Later, Randy was appointed Ray Sanders' youth director, then he later became state overseer of Minnesota. Ray mentored Randy, and Randy has mentored hundreds of others.

On their way to Minnesota, the team stopped in Michigan City, Indiana, with Pastor Larry Pemberton for a weekend meeting. From the start, God seemed to set His approval on the invasion by adding 14 souls to the kingdom of God that weekend. When they arrived in Minnesota, they worked in churches in Bloomington, St. Paul, Duluth, Chisholm, Southside, Minneapolis and Rochester. That summer they visited 5,726 homes, passed out 6,490 tracts and contacted 2,346 people. There were 210 prospects for the churches, and 73 people prayed to receive salvation. Randy wrote these verses in his journal concerning that summer: "How shall they believe in him of whom they have not heard? and how shall they hear without a preacher? And how shall they preach, except they be sent? as it is written, How beautiful are the feet of them that preach the gospel of peace, and bring glad tidings of good things!" (Romans 10:14, 15).

That invasion had its challenges and stresses. Toward the end of the invasion there was a major problem. Randy had sent students out to witness. He and Tom stayed in the room because they needed to prepare their sermons. The stress had gotten to them. After awhile together, they got into an actual fight, nearly tearing the room apart. Then they had to get up and preach that night.

Randy went back to Lee College after that summer. He met Kathy Flynn. They were sitting in Shoney's restaurant talking about the future. Kathy asked Randy what were his goals. He said, "I want to work with Ray Sanders. I want to build a church. I want to be a state youth director." When he went to pay his bill, there stood Ray Sanders, state overseer of Minnesota. Ray asked him about coming to Minnesota to be his state youth director.

In 1976, Randy and Kathy, now married, went to Minnesota to serve as state youth director. They stayed seven years. In 1990, they returned as state overseer and are still serving in that capacity.

Charles loved the Hamons. He kept them encouraged. Often he called and said, "I'm proud of you." He came to visit them often and ministered in their churches all over Minnesota. In 1991, Randy sent Charles to speak in a church in Grasston, pastored by his brother-in-law, Michael Flynn. Michael's church was very small at the time. But Charles took him to a nursing home. They went room-to-room and led two older women to the Lord that afternoon. Michael's life was revolutionized. Today his church averages 250 people, and he credits his church growth to his encounter with Charles Beach.

Charles spoke at camp meetings on several occasions, but he would never take an honorarium. On one occasion Randy insisted that he take an honorarium. He refused and said, "I am giving this to your family. Write me and tell me what you do with it." They bought a camping tent and had many wonderful family outings.

When Ray Sanders was overseer of Minnesota, he took Randy under his care and transferred the gifts he had in him to Randy. Thus, Randy Hamon and his beautiful and gifted wife, Kathy, followed the Sanders and have had a double-portion anointing for the work of God there.

What God Can Do Through One Man

D.L. Moody once said, "The world has yet to see what God can do with one man who is totally dedicated to Him." Charles Beach was that man—totally surrendered to God in every area of his life. He set the course for evangelism in the Church of God for generations.

6

LAY MINISTER OF EVANGELISM

In 1971, Charles became the minister of evangelism at the North Cleveland Church of God, while still serving as professor at Lee College. Dr. T.L. Lowery was the pastor at that time. This made history, because he was the first Church of God layman to be hired in a ministry position. "Because of his outstanding abilities, we were able to establish outreach chapels all over the greater Cleveland area," said Lowery. Charles took full responsibility for the East Cleveland Chapel. He bused the children in and brought adults in his own car. Whatever it took to get people to that chapel and to God, he did it.

Divine Connections

During this time, God brought Leonard Albert to Cleveland. He had been led to the Lord by Teresa (Patricia) Peters, who became his wife. Teresa Peters was a lifetime resident of Mattawamkeag, Maine. She had gone to Lee College and became a powerful Pioneers for Christ leader. She was in the great Dillon (South Carolina) invasion, and worked in Salt Lake City, Barbados and a number of other great invasions. But the impact of PFC went far beyond those weekend invasions and summer witnessing teams. After graduation, this soulwinning zeal did not diminish.

In 1968 when Teresa went home to get a job, Leonard Albert hired her as his secretary at Barrows Transport Company in Portland, Maine. The truck drivers in the company did not know how to act with a lady around. Leonard started liking this young lady.

After a few weeks, Teresa invited him to go to church with her. Fearfully, he agreed to go. What a service! This was not only Leonard's introduction to Christ, but he was also introduced to a great Pentecostal outpouring. The power of God fell, and people were speaking in tongues. One man even came up to Leonard and gave him a big hug. In Leonard's social circles, this was totally unacceptable. But somehow it seemed OK. He returned with Teresa to church. He also began watching Christian television and listening to gospel music. Conviction was gripping his heart.

Teresa had been a leader in winning the lost in Pioneers for Christ, but she had no idea that she was winning a great trainer of soulwinners to Christ. One night, Leonard got alone in his bedroom and cried out, "God, if You're really up there [he didn't know if God was up there or not], save me." It happened just that easily. He knew God had changed his life. This was the pivotal point in his life—he would never be the same.

Soon Leonard realized he was in love with Teresa. After they were married, they moved to Newfoundland. God spoke to Leonard to go to Lee College. He arrived in 1970, but he did not meet Charles personally until 1971.

The day he met Charles Beach in the lobby of the North Cleveland Church of God was one of the greatest moments for Church of God lay ministries. Leonard had only been saved for about two years and was struggling with his call to Christian service. He was trying to figure out how he was to live his life for Christ.

Theirs was a relationship born in heaven. From this time on, the story of Charles Beach in soulwinning was greatly shared by Leonard Albert. Charles became his mentor, convincing Leonard that he could be a minister, regardless of whether or not he had credentials.

The Lord revealed to Leonard that he was called to lay ministry. Charles was there for him as he had been there for thousands of others in his lifetime. Just as Charles mentored Leonard and hundreds of others, Leonard has mentored thousands of others.

Training Others in His Gifts

Charles taught Leonard how to witness to people. "He gave me a copy *of Evangelism Explosion,* by Dr. James Kennedy, and my life hasn't been the same since," Leonard said.

While attending Lee, Leonard worked for Cleveland Chair Company as a traffic manager for two and a half years. He began his evangelism mentorship under Charles Beach while he was working.

Up until this time Leonard did not know people could be saved outside the church. The first time Charles took Leonard out to witness was quite an experience. They went to the home of Lucille Ash. When they arrived at the house, there was a dog. Mrs. Ash said, "Don't worry about the dog. She won't bite." Charles began telling Mrs. Ash about what Jesus could do in her life. But Leonard was having a problem. While his mentor was having a good ole time witnessing to this lady, the dog bit Leonard. That "dog that wouldn't bite" bit Leonard on the leg through his trousers. He wanted to let out a blood-curdling scream. He wanted to kick the dog in the teeth, but he did not want to interrupt his mentor. The leg hurt. Leonard was angry! He wanted to choke the dog, but Charles continued witnessing. While he was in excruciating pain, Leonard watched his mentor lead this woman to the Lord.

Later, he had to go to the hospital and get a tetanus shot. Years later Leonard affirms that this dog bite was the trick of the Enemy to get him off course. The devil would have liked to have turned one of God's future greatest soul-winners sour on door-to-door witnessing. Since this time he has knocked on literally thousands of doors and has never been bitten by a dog again.

Later Leonard and Charles went back and led Lucille's husband, Grover Ash, to the Lord. Grover's arm had been severed from the shoulder. Later, when the gas station where he worked was robbed, Grover was killed.

While Leonard was working with Charles, he continued his job. Even there he had picked up so much of the philosophy of Charles Beach—his mentor. When there was no janitor at his place of employment, Leonard cleaned the rest rooms. The boss liked that and gave him a promotion.

The Trainee Became a Servant

As Leonard watched Charles, he understood that the heart of a true leader of God is servanthood, and servanthood is the catalyst for increasing the anointing. *Anointing* means "responsibility," and responsibility leads to leadership. Leonard became committed to Charles and he began to serve him. During this time he realized that Charles needed a relaxing chair for his office. So he bought him a comfortable executive chair. This began to bond a friendship that would last all their lives together. Every Christmas Leonard bought his mentor a suit and took it to his home. But then Charles would figure out how much the suit cost and pay tithes on that amount.

Developing the Church s Witnessing Program

Leonard was assigned the job of developing the witnessing program at North Cleveland under Charles' supervision. Only four people were involved at the first meeting, besides Leonard: Ken Pike, Jerry Huntley, Dennis Threadgill and Benny Pittman (who was on staff at North Cleveland). Leonard was discouraged, but not Charles! He began to boast of their having four people. Then Leonard began to realize the significance of small beginnings.

Charles organized people to visit all day every Saturday for the bus and chapel ministries of North Cleveland. Charles would not permit these workers to use rain or other foul weather as a deterrent. They developed every kind of evangelism tool that was possible. There was door-to-door witnessing, a "sonshine" wagon and puppet shows.

99

Eight chapels were organized. Mobile homes were located everywhere, so they put chapels right in the midst of them.

Charles valued commitment. He told the workers, "We will give account for Acts 1:8. God gave us the Holy Spirit so that we can be witnesses."

During this period of time, Charles personally won hundreds to the Lord. He often said, "When any person comes to Jesus, that person is responding to a drawing of God's Holy Spirit and is, therefore, never ever hopelessly lost (see John 6:44). When that person responds to the drawing and wooing of God's Holy Ghost and comes to Jesus, Jesus never ever turns him or her away (see v. 37). When that person comes to the Lord, calls upon Him and penitently confesses his sins, he is saved. God's Word says that he is saved (1 John 1:9), and God cannot lie (Titus 1:2; Hebrews 6:18)."

He taught the workers that every person you meet is a divine appointment. He said, "If you can't get the whole family, start with one. Then the others will come." Soon North Cleveland workers were leading entire families to Christ.

He Loved the Poor

Charles Beach loved the poor. He wrote an article for the *Evangel* (Sept. 13, 1971) that stated his philosophy about the poor. He titled it "The Other Sign Following."

God had permitted John to baptize Jesus, had spoken to him from heaven, and had allowed him to see the Holy Ghost descending like a dove upon Christ. John had recognized the Messiah and had forcefully declared, "Behold the Lamb of God, which taketh away the sin of the world" (John 1:29). Yet after John was put in prison, he was oppressed of the devil and became so discouraged that he even began to doubt that Jesus was the Christ. In fact, He sent two of His disciples to Jesus to ask: "Art thou he that should come, or do we look for another?" (Matthew 11:3). Jesus said unto them, "Go your way, and tell John what things ye have seen and heard; how that the blind see [this miracle confirms My messiahship], . . . the lepers are cleansed [this miracle confirms My messiahship], . . . the dead are raised [this miracle confirms My messiahship], and to the poor the gospel is preached [this miracle—that other sign following—also confirms My messiahship]" (Luke 7:22).

Mr. Beach went on to write these words: "Too many of the sign-seeking believers of this closing 20 century have almost totally forgotten 'that other sign following.' They have begun to neglect the ghettos' poor and the slums' suffering—the inner city."

Charles was determined for the North Cleveland Evangelism Department to not neglect the city's poor.

Evangelism to the Nursing Homes

Even though the North Cleveland Church was vitally important to him, as well as the Pioneers for Christ at Lee College, he did not neglect the nursing homes during this time.

Cory Ledsford was 80 years old. Charles witnessed to her almost every day. When she cursed him and told him to get out, Charles always responded, "Jesus loves you. You don't have to go to hell." One day he went in and found her crying. "What's wrong?" he asked. "I don't want to go to hell." Charles led her to the Lord. Shortly thereafter she went to be with the Lord. But Charles knew where she went, because he had prayed that simple sinner's prayer with her.

Witnessing to the Cultists in Cleveland

Charles witnessed to Jehovah's Witnesses everywhere he could find them. When they would not listen to him, he would say, "Torment! Torment! That's what hell is."

Still Working for the Church After Promotion

Charles Beach was later appointed secretary of lay affairs and officially left the North Cleveland staff. However, he continued to work with them in soulwinning efforts. Leonard followed him as evangelism director, then Mitch Maloney came on board under the pastorate of Ronnie Brock. These three men became a trio for establishing evangelism in the North Cleveland area. They trained over 1,000 people in evangelism at the North Cleveland Church of God. To this day soulwinning classes are a regular part of the church—the legacy of Dr. Charles Beach.

Mitch worked the housing projects. His assignment was to visit every house in the projects every week. The North Cleveland Church rented the Pathfinder's Chapel— a four-bedroom house near the projects. One Sunday a lady brought her four kids. Mitch preached the worst sermon he had ever preached. He knew it. But the lady responded to the altar call. She was saved. In nine months, the chapel was filled with 97 people. At the same time

Charles was still working the East Side Chapel on Eighth Street.

Mitch got settled in the North Cleveland Church of God as evangelism director, but God spoke to him and said, "Don't become too comfortable." Mitch then felt led to go to Detroit to begin a new work. He took the methods he had been taught and went door-to-door. The weather was cold in Detroit, but soon a great church was born. The Maloneys stayed there 15 years and then returned to pastor the North Cleveland Church of God.

7

LAYMAN OF THE CENTURY AT WORK

The man who has led more people to Christ than any individual in the Church of God is a layman—Charles! Leland Smelser said, "This layman lit a flame of evangelism which consumed the hearts of thousands."

Charles received many tributes, but the most meaningful to him and most definitive of his life's goals was when the Church of God named him Layman of the Century at the Centennial General Assembly in 1986.

In 1964, Church of God General Overseer Wade H. Horton appointed the first lay committee. Charles Beach was named to that committee.

During the 1966-68 biennium, the National Laymen's Committee was called the National Layman's Board. Charles was a member of that board. Reverend Houston Morehead was brought in to be the director of Men's Fellowship. Charles' student and PFC leader, Aubrey Maye, was appointed the first Pioneers for Christ field representative. His job was to coordinate students working with summer witness teams, as well as to help churches develop local PFC witnessing groups. This program was phased out in 1970.

In 1972 a part-time office was opened with Charles serving as part-time lay affairs representative and full-time professor at Lee College.

In 1975 Leonard Albert, Charles' sidekick, was also added as part-time Men's Fellowship field representative to help train laymen to witness. Pastor Ronnie Brock was pleased with Leonard and did not want to lose him. He asked Charles who was being considered for this new position. Charles said, "Leonard is at the top of the list." Ronnie asked, "Who else is on the list?" "Leonard Albert, Leonard Albert and Leonard Albert," Charles replied.

Training laymen of the Church of God to be witnesses—using the same techniques he had used to turn Lee College into a soulwinning campus—was the heartthrob of Charles Beach. He often said, "Do you realize what could happen if we could get laymen turned on to soulwinning? If each layman in the Church of God could win one person, and that one win one, the world could be won in 33 years." And he went to work on that project. He talked to every layman who would listen to him about winning the harvest.

Full-Time Secretary of Lay Affairs

In 1976 Charles was named full-time secretary of lay affairs. At this time, lay affairs was a part of the Evangelism and Home Missions Department.

Many people recognized Charles Beach was serving in the position for which he was born. Even the Bradley County sheriff wrote him a letter of congratulations when he was appointed full-time to the lay office. This was the pivotal moment of Charles' life. From this office, he would affect the Church of God to become a soulwinning church as no other man ever did.

The objectives of this office were basically to mobilize the laity of the Church of God to do four things:

1. Back the pastor
2. Support the church
3. Be better witnesses
4. Become more generous stewards to God's cause

"We have seen the Church of God make a major turn toward personal witnessing since we began training our laymen to do it," Charles said. "However, the victories we are now celebrating could not have been accomplished without ministerial leaders like Wade H. Horton, Ray H. Hughes, Cecil B. Knight, T.L. Lowery, Raymond Crowley and John Nichols."

For years the real thrust in evangelism had been mass revivals. But Charles believed that along with mass revivals there should be a renewal of witnessing on a one-to-one basis.

Charles expressed his beliefs strongly: "People—men, women, and children, old and young in every race and color—die by the multitudes every single day and go to hell, but not just because they are sinners. These people die and go to hell, unfortunately, because the laborers in His harvest are ever, ever so few." He set out to change things.

Charles was often disappointed in the philosophy of many pastors. "Come to church, pay tithes, don't cause trouble" was often what he picked up from pastors. He often shouted, "If you have the baptism of the Holy Spirit and you're not witnessing, you are failing God. It sounds harsh, but that's what it's for."

Evangelism Breakthrough Manual

Charles liked the pattern of evangelism used by Dr. James Kennedy and the Coral Ridge Presbyterian Church in Fort Lauderdale, Florida. Dr. Kennedy had written about their soulwinning methods in *Evangelism Explosion*. Kennedy had been a young discouraged pastor, but his life was changed when he ministered for a pastor in Decatur, Georgia, in a 10-day evangelistic campaign. He accompanied the pastor each day—morning and afternoon—in his home-visitation and witnessing program. In a 10-day period Kennedy watched the Decatur pastor lead 54 persons to Christ. Kennedy told how he returned to Fort Lauderdale and began the same type of witnessing program with astonishing results. Kennedy mobilized his laity by taking them out with him (one at a time) to witness a sufficient number of times to develop self-confidence in witnessing to others. After these laymen were trained—had on-the-job training—they in turn trained others.

John Nichols, director of evangelism, said, "Let's do our own manual." In 1972 while only a part-time staff member at the Lay Affairs office and with Dr. Kennedy's blessing, Charles set out to put *Evangelism Explosion* into a form Church of God laymen could use—*Evangelism Breakthrough*. Charles really believed this was a breakthrough method for us, even though he had patterned it after Dr. James Kennedy. *Evangelism Breakthrough* spoke to our laity. Now that he was a full-time staff member, he was ready to go.

Training Lay Witnesses

Charles said, "This is the way it ought to be—every layman a witness! He set out to instill this philosophy into the laymen of the Church of God. He wanted *Evangelism Breakthrough* to do for laymen what Pioneers for Christ had done for Lee College. Students had been great at witnessing, but they were in churches and cities for only a short time. Laymen were there to stay. He had a vision. It started to work. One Canadian pastor caught the vision. During the first eight months of implementing this program, 103 new members were added to his church. This pastor said, "This is the most revolutionary technique for personal evangelism in the 20th century to mobilize the sleeping giant of our laity."

Evangelism Breakthrough classes were taught throughout the nation. Charles and Leonard Albert went to hundreds of churches and taught them how to reach their city for Christ. They taught pastors how to conduct their own training classes. Pastor Larry Bond, who was then pastor in Benton, Illinois, said, "This lay evangelism program has set our church on fire for God. It's exciting to see new converts coming to church. Without exception, everyone who has become a trainee who did not have the baptism of the Holy Ghost has received it." One man that had sought the Baptism for 24 years received the Holy Ghost.

One 75-year-old man, who had attended church all his life, was saved in his home when the gospel was presented. He could not bring himself to go to the altar at church. "I wondered if I could keep people coming for 16 weeks, but they seldom ever missed. We had 12 trainers and trainees the first term, and we had 18 the second term. Five who were won through this program entered as trainees and are now winning others for God," Bond said.

"Remarks such as 'I never felt fulfilled as a Christian until I got involved in *Evangelism Breakthrough*' and 'I feel closer to God than I ever did before' are often heard from the trainees and trainers alike."

As people began to be open and respond to the *Evangelism Breakthrough* program, the results were unbelievable. Churches began realizing they could really win the lost. It was easy. It was fun!

Films Developed to Challenge Laymen

Shortly after coming on board in the lay office, Charles was given the task of developing three films for the Evangelism Department. They were *Jimmy Doesn't Know Jesus, Evangelism Breakthrough*, and a film on men's fellowship.

Developing Soulwinning Materials

Beach felt that soulwinning had to become the primary job of this office. He felt that he had to furnish them with good witnessing materials. He set out to develop materials for children, youth, adult and senior adults, cults, and any other area of evangelism he could imagine. His goal was not to flood pastors and laymen with ineffective programs, because he realized churches were busy already. His desire was to provide the very best witnessing and outreach materials, so they might become involved in the one great objective of the Lord Jesus: to seek and to save that which was lost.

Until this time, Charles' ministry had been training students to take the gospel to the ends of the earth. Now his ministry began to cover the entire age spectrum—the PFC for the young people, the lay office for church middle-age group, and a program of prayer, shut-in and nursing home visitation for senior adults. He had a passion to do for the laity what he had done for Lee College students. However, he knew that college students could only be in one place for a short period of time. Laity could remain in the local church and community. He foresaw that he could make an even greater impact by pouring his life into dedicated laymen. He traveled around the country to implement the program. He also began writing materials for all of these areas. He wrote and published the *Laymen's Quarterly Bulletin*, which provided information and news of successful soulwinning men's fellowships and programs sponsored by the Lay Affairs Department. Early in 1977 he organized the first overseas lay seminar. From that point on, laymen all over the world were turned on to soulwinning.

School of Lay Evangelism

The first lay witnessing school was kicked off in Cleveland, Tennessee, October 21-25, 1977, with over 200 registered. It was a time of intensive training and witnessing in over 800 homes with 44 conversions.

Then in October 1980, Charles and Leonard Albert initiated Phase II of the School of Lay Evangelism. Built on Phase I, this program added cult witnessing, lay apologetics, a discipleship class, counseling and outreach ministries.

Mitch Maloney was brought in to help with many of the soulwinning classes. They took laymen into the harvest, dramatizing sermons on the streets. Often 5,000 homes were visited a day. It was not unusual for 50 to 125 people to be saved as a result of these witnessing endeavors.

During almost all of these training seminars and schools, Charles was scouting out the territory while the other men were teaching the laymen. He always had the area laid out and waiting for the witnessing teams.

Then he, too, always took people out to witness. You might think he looked for the sharpest men to train. But for some reason, he always looked for the handicapped. If someone was crippled, blind or feeble, that's who Charles chose to work with. He loved to see the joy of a handicapped person leading someone to Jesus.

Bermuda was one of the many places where Charles took a lady out who was in a wheelchair. He pushed her wheelchair from house to house, and together they led a soul to Christ.

National Lay Witness Week

Through the *Laymen's Quarterly Bulletin*, Charles began making appeals for evangelism. He suggested that during National Lay Witness Week laymen do the following:

- Find someone in prison (or jail) and "come unto him" with 1 John 1:9.

- Find someone sick (in a hospital, in a nursing home) and visit him or her with Acts 16:31.

- Find someone spiritually "hungered" in the several blocks around your home (or church) and give him the "Son" of John 3:16, "the living bread which . . . if any man eat . . he shall live for ever" (6:51).

- Find some spiritually "naked" children, start a kid's club, and clothe them with the love and gospel of Him who said, "Suffer the little children to come unto me, and forbid them not: for of such is the kingdom of God" (Mark 10:14).

- Find some "stranger," a shut-in in your town or city—thirsty for the blessings you enjoy daily—and take him or her to the light of fellowship of 1 John 1:7 to drink of the water that Jesus shall give him so he will never thirst.

Charles challenged his students to make the soulwinning ministries a part of their daily life—supplying some of the physical and material needs of those to whom they ministered. Then on that great day, Jesus will say to you, "Come, ye blessed of my Father, inherit the kingdom prepared for you" (Matthew 25:34; read vv. 31-46).

Ministering Locally While Ministering to the Nations

In addition to his rigorous duties at the General Offices, Charles still took time to visit the hospital every night, worked in the bus ministry of the North Cleveland Church of God, and led seminars for Lee College Pioneers for Christ.

While serving the Lay Department, Charles was determined not to be a lay witness in name only. He witnessed to or visited 100 people every day. Hospital visitation was part of his daily routine.

"Witnessing is the job and obligation of every Christian, and should not be neglected because of fear, insecurity or inferiority," Charles maintained. He continued, "I believe soulwinning is the most important work in the world. Anytime you get someone to accept the Lord, it's eternal."

Conducted His Personal Tract Brigades

Passing out tracts was a natural part of his lifestyle. Dr. Bryan Cutshall, the present pastor of Twin Rivers Worship

Center in St. Louis, tells about being influenced by this lifestyle evangelism method. Dr. Cutshall writes: "Once I was traveling upstate and made regular stops along the way to fill up with gas and get a bite to eat. On one trip I came across three gospel tracts in three different men's rest rooms that had been left on the sink. On the back was stamped the address of the North Cleveland Church of God. Without asking, I knew I was traveling the same route that day as Charles. When I arrived at the conference, he was there. I asked him which route he took. Sure enough, I was following his breadcrumb trail to Calvary. That very next week, I bought my own tracts to start handing out. I never told him he is the reason I started doing that."

He Witnessed Everywhere

Kathy Sanders casually mentioned to Charles that her mother had remarried. Her stepfather's brother who lived in Muleshoe, Texas, had cancer and was unsaved. On his next trip to Salt Lake City, Charles got off I-20 Highway and traveled 200 miles out of his way to go to Muleshoe. Since he had no address, he began asking people, "Do you know a farmer who has cancer?" He finally met somebody who knew who he was talking about. Charles knocked on this total stranger's door, told him who he was and led him to Jesus. He did not even tell Kathy about the experience. She learned about it when her stepfather called and asked, "Do you know a man named Beach?" Then he told her the story of his brother's conversion. This is true religion—undefiled.

Nursing Homes

In October 1985 with the help of Mount Olive Church of God Evangelism Outreach, Charles sponsored a fun day for the residents of Life Care Center of Cleveland. They toured the outside of the facility aboard a hay wagon. At the end of the journey, they sat by a fire on blanket-covered bales of hay for a hotdog/marshmallow roast. Twenty-five Pioneers for Christ members from Lee College led them in singing some favorite hymns.

Charles knew seniors like 105-year-old Granny Howard. This bright and blue-eyed lady said she had won at least eight or nine people to the Lord in the nursing home where she had been a patient for several years. Charles called her the World's Oldest Soulwinner.

The Church of God Men's Fellowships combined with Ladies Ministries set aside the last Sunday in May as Senior Citizens Day to honor or visit the elderly in private homes, nursing homes or housing projects.

When traveling, Charles would drive until he felt led of the Lord to stop. He would check into a Motel 6 or an economy motel or sleep in his Rambler. Then he would find a nursing home to visit. He would go from room to room spreading cheer and leading people to the Lord.

8

How to Witness to the Aged

There are many different ways Christians can be a witness to the older members in their communities. One of the most effective ways to help the aged find Christ is to visit a nursing home or "old folks home."

The following steps, written by Betty Robbins, will show how to prepare for a witnessing service in a nursing home.

1. *The home.* Choose the nursing home you think has the greatest need. Contact the supervisor well in advance to receive permission to visit and witness in the home. Plan the complete service at least a week ahead. Several days before the service, ask those whom you wish to participate in the service. Inform the singers in ample time for them to practice before the service. Advise the speaker to speak slowly and loud enough for the elderly people to hear and understand the message. Assign several people the responsibility of giving a personal

testimony about the reality of Christ in their lives. Give each of them an outline of your plans for the service.

2. *The services.* Two types of services can be held in a nursing home. The first type is one where all the patients are in one room. A number of songs can be used in this type of service, with the patients participating if possible. Since it will be necessary for the supervisor to assemble the people in a certain room at a certain time each week, it is imperative to always be on time.

The second type of service was preferred by the members of the Lee College Pioneers for Christ club. In this service the aged are visited individually in their private rooms by two or three persons. This service affords a much better opportunity for personal witnessing. These teams of two or three persons go from room to room each week, keeping the following things in mind:

- Learn each person by name.

- Try to visit the same ones each week; listen to their problems, offer consolation and encouragement.

- Be cheerful.

- Let the old folks know you love them. Many of them will never have visitors—not even from their own families.

- Read to them from God's Word. It is best to ask them if they have a special verse of Scripture they would like you to read.

- Be sure to pray with them about their particular problems, desires and needs. Ask them for permission to pray; do not infringe upon their rights, and avoid upsetting the extremely ill by praying too loudly.

- Sing a well-known hymn softly to them or with them.

- Last, and most important of all, try to lead them to Christ if it is apparent that they are not saved. You may follow the formula suggested in "How to Lead a Soul to Christ" for this part of the service.

These same steps may be followed when visiting and witnessing to the aged in individual homes. Remember, the aged need Christ. They need you to bring Him to them. They are nearer eternity than anyone else.

Charles had a burden for seeing that the aging were helped. Therefore the department started SAFE (the Senior Adult Fellowship Endeavor).

Ministry to Cults

Charles loved to witness to the cults, especially Mormons and Jehovah's Witnesses. He spent hours researching the cults and wrote numerous tracts and several books on witnessing to the cults, including *What Jehovah Wants His Witnesses to Know* and *How to Witness to Mormons*. He learned everything he knew about the cults the hard way—by just going out and doing it. He often went to the nursing homes and looked for people who belonged to cults.

Stella Hill was a Jehovah's Witness. He visited her every day and told her about Jesus. He even took his daughter, Sharlinda, to see her. Then one day Charles and Leonard led this dying woman to Jesus. When the Witnesses left the *Watchtower* in her room, she responded, "Why are they leaving this stuff around here?" When she died, Charles and Leonard Albert went to the funeral at the Kingdom Hall. Not a tear was shed by anybody. Leonard turned to Charles and wept. "They got her body; but we got her soul," he said.

Judy Rogers was another Jehovah's Witness whom Charles led to the Lord. He had knocked on her door numerous times, only to be cussed out. But Charles was persistent. He did not want her to go to hell. One day he received a call from Judy. "I am in the hospital. I have melanoma cancer." He went to the hospital and led her to Jesus. She cried, "Can I have a Christmas tree now for my family this Christmas? Can I celebrate my son's birthday?" One day God took her home, but she died with a fantastic testimony of the saving power of the Lord.

Mormons were a great burden of Charles Beach. He developed an interesting study on their teachings and practices regarding the Temple garments.

During one of his trips to Salt Lake City to witness to Mormons, he stood outside the Mormon Temple. As Mormon church leaders filed out, he began to witness to them. After listening for several minutes, one of their leaders exclaimed, "Why, you know more about the *Book of Mormon* than I do!"

Charles had such a burden for the Mormons that he put his church membership in the Ogden, Utah, Church of God. He sent them his tithes to help support their ministry. When a breakthrough came, Charles and Lois Beach felt that they had a vital part in it because they had poured money into the Ogden church. Several outstanding men of God, including Bob Blackaby and the Pioneers for Christ, pastored the church and laid groundwork for a break-through. When Rocky Schrable was pastoring there, a lady was healed and that started the turnaround for the work of God there. Many times when Charles and Leonard would go there, 200 people would be in the services—a miracle of God in a Mormon city.

"If you want to get a cultist saved, you must get him to investigate the Scriptures," said Charles. "The Word is the sword of the Spirit. Put that Word into their minds and the Holy Spirit will work on the individual." He further taught, "The best way to witness to a cultist is to find one of the cult's major doctrines that is not supported by its own Bible. The Jehovah's Witnesses deny the deity of Christ. I memorized five scriptures that show Jesus is God, but I found I couldn't use the King James Version because they disregard it as the Word of God. So, I bought their Bibles, the *New World Translation* and the *Kingdom Interlinear*. Their own Bibles contradict what they teach."

Charles developed materials and seminars on how to witness to the cults. He and Leonard Albert did a skit on how to witness to Jehovah's Witnesses. Leonard played the part of the Jehovah's Witness. It was so real that people thought he was a genuine cultist. People would get upset and call him a "two-legged demon" and "a devil." One time Leonard said to Charles, "I am tired of being called a devil." Charles responded, "You're a natural. Besides, you are the best devil we have."

Leonard often tells of the horrible nightmare in a prayer conference in North Georgia in 1982. He and Charles taught the morning Bible study. Right in the middle of their Jehovah's Witness skit, a retired pastor became convinced that Leonard was in fact a real cultist. He got up right in the middle of their skit and yelled, "Why doesn't someone set that donkey [the other name used in Georgia] down!" From that day on, Leonard was often affectionately called Jack Albert.

Conquering the Fear of Flying

Even though Charles and Leonard went to numerous cities and countries, Charles always drove because he had a fear of flying. They traveled together for thousands of miles in that Rambler station wagon. If he could not drive, he would go by ship. His fear of flying came when he was a child. A one-man plane had crashed in their backyard in Texas and the pilot burned to death. An uncle had taken him to the funeral. It made such an impression on Charles as a young child he never wanted to be near an airplane. Then when he was in the Navy, he hated the sound of the planes that flew into the ships, destroying the lives of many of his friends.

However, the day came when he had to fly. The Evangelism Department scheduled a conference in Puerto Rico in 1977. Charles had tried to get passage on every ship he could find. Nothing was available. Charles threw a pencil across the room. "Every door is closed," he exclaimed. He had to fly. Even though Lois was not going on the trip, she boarded the plane in Chattanooga with Charles. She sat beside him, held his hand and assured him that the plane would be safe. Dr. Delton Alford, who was sitting across the aisle, thought Charles was sick because he prayed all the way. He would have refused to make the trip had it not been for John Nichols and the appreciation he had for all he was doing for laymen in the church.

When he arrived at the airport, Leonard was there to meet him. When Charles put his feet on the ground, he began to shout, "I made it! I made it!" This conquered his fear of flying.

But as always, the Enemy has his plot ready. When one man saw Charles shouting for joy, he said, "Be glad you were on that plane. The engine on our plane caught fire and we had to go back to land." This was another attempt to put Charles in bondage so he could not travel to do the work of God. But the Enemy lost. He got on the plane to return, and kept flying until the Lord took him home.

His Kindness Sometimes Created Problems

Sometimes Charles' kindness and desire to see souls saved created problems for him. One thing he needed was his privacy. But he loved the American Indians. Once while driving through Cortez, Colorado, he picked up a couple of Indians. He soon discovered that they did not speak English or Spanish or any of the other languages he spoke. All they did was grunt. When he stopped to get gas, he told the attendant, "I picked up these two Indians, but I don't know where they are going." The man responded, "They will ride with you forever wherever you go. You better leave them here and let them get back home." So Charles bought them food and gave them money and went his way. He often wondered what happened to those Indians. *Were they saved?*

High Goals

He developed programs such as Lay Witness Week and Laymen's Literature for the Lost. He set high goals for the laymen. The goal for the department in 1982 was twofold.

1. Make 2 million contacts through family to family, house to house, institution, or other forms of witnessing by Church of God lay workers around the world.

2. Reach over 3 million unsaved souls in India through the distribution of gospel tracts provided by Church of God Men's Fellowships and lay witnesses.

Charles and Leonard believed in the duplication principle. Charles trained Leonard Albert. Leonard trained laymen such as Hollis Allred, self-described as a "disgruntled, unhappy Mississippi layman." Hollis started several nursing home Sunday schools and put laymen to work teaching the Word. In one of these outreach Sunday schools, he invited the nursing home owner to church. She came, was converted, joined the church and became a tither. Her sister came, was converted and became a tither.

Mr. Allred taught Sunday school for four months in a county jail before winning a young drug pusher to the Lord who had a 15-year sentence. The young man, Doug Fisher, was released after his conversion. What a thrill to see him receive the Holy Spirit baptism and join the Natchez Church of God. Charles had won Leonard Albert; Leonard trained Hollis Allred. Hollis won and trained Doug Fisher. Doug became a minister of the gospel. He had 13 saved and six filled with the Holy Ghost in his first revival.

Writing to Help Laymen

Charles began writing materials to teach laymen how to witness effectively. Included in his writings are the following: *The Lay Coordinator's Manual, Evangelism Breakthrough,*

What Jehovah Wants His Witnesses to Know, The Not So Amazing Mormonism, and *What the Layman Needs to Know in Order to Deal With the Cults.*

Impact Rallies and Speaking to the Nations

In 1975 the Evangelism and Home Missions Department implemented the Impact Rallies. Charles taught in 60 of these rallies across the nation, which greatly increased lay involvement throughout the United States.

He taught over 100 schools on lay evangelism. He spoke to the nations, lecturing on all phases of personal evangelism and cult evangelism in Korea, Philippines, Argentina, Mexico, El Salvador, Guatemala, Puerto Rico, Bermuda, Barbados, Jamaica, Haiti, Tortola, France, Germany, England, Hawaii, Alaska and Canada. He spoke on evangelism in all the 50 states except South Dakota, Vermont and New Hampshire. However, he sent his representatives—his students—to even those states.

In 1977 he and Leonard went to Santiago, Dominican Republic, for a men's rally. Andres Rincon, evangelism director, had scheduled the meeting in a basketball stadium. There were more than 3,000 men in that meeting and many, many of them were saved. The laity and ministers were challenged to get involved in the harvest.

Charles was not one to merely lecture about soulwinning. He did it. If he and Lois stopped at a gasoline station, she knew before they left he would give out tracts and ask if the attendants were saved. If they ate in a restaurant, she knew he would give a tract to somebody and ask if he or she knew the Lord. If he bought something in a store, she knew he would give the clerk a tract and ask her if she had ever been born again.

125

Passion for Pastors

He had a love for pastors. John Lombard said, "As a young pastor, I knew Charles was praying for me daily and was with me at the time of my greatest need. He drove 150 miles to be with me and I'll never forget it."

Men's Fellowship Manifesto

Charles developed lectures and wrote articles concerning how laymen should treat their pastor. He wrote the following Men's Fellowship Manifesto.

I am a Church of God layman.

As a Church of God layman, I have, first of all, a solemn obligation to support my church and to back my pastor in every soulwinning endeavor that he undertakes (1 Corinthians 4:2).

As a Church of God layman, I have a solemn obligation to pray for my pastor-shepherd every single day (1 Timothy 2:1, 2).

As a Church of God layman, I have a solemn obligation to back my pastor with my tithes and offerings. If I do not, I am robbing God (Malachi 3:8-10; Matthew 23:23).

As a Church of God layman, I have an obligation to let my pastor know that I love and appreciate him and his ministry (1 Thessalonians 5:12, 13).

As a Church of God layman, I have an obligation to offer to assist my pastor in his visitation program in hospitals, nursing homes and elderly housing projects (Acts 5:42).

As a Church of God layman, I have an obligation to help my pastor in the bus ministry and in the inception of branch Sunday schools (Luke 14:21-23).

As a Church of God layman, I have an obligation to help my pastor in his house-to-house witnessing program (Acts 20:20).

If I, a Church of God layman, do not fulfill these obligations, if I do not witness for Christ, then "I am a hearer of the Word and not a doer, deceiving myself" (see James 1:22).

If I, a Church of God layman, do not witness for Christ, then my faith, having no works, being alone, is absolutely dead (James 2:17).

If I, a Church of God layman, fail to witness for Christ, it is because I am filled with my own ways and am therefore a backslider in heart (Proverbs 14:14; James 4:17).

If I, a Church of God layman, fail to witness to the poor lost souls of this world, whom I should love, then I have lost my first love and the Lord has somewhat against me (Revelation 2:4).

If I, a Church of God layman, fail to witness for Christ and do not the works of the Lord, then my "heart goeth after covetousness," while I show love only with my lips (Ezekiel 33:30-33).

If I, a Church of God layman, fail to witness for Christ and fail to save others "with fear, pulling them out of the fire," then I help to usher these same precious souls into an eternal, everlasting, non-ending, tormenting hell (Jude 23).

But I cannot, I must not fail. As a Church of God layman in these last days just before the imminent return of the Lord, I cannot afford to become at ease in Zion (Amos 6:1).

Many, many people in this country are satisfied because they are free from tyranny and oppression. Many, many

Christians are satisfied because they are free from the penalty of sin.

But may God grant that I, as a Church of God layman, never ever be satisfied until I can say, like Paul, "I am free and pure from the blood of all men" (Acts 20:26).

—Charles Beach

Lay Coordinator's Manual

In 1980 Charles felt the need for local churches to have a lay coordinator. He realized pastors are too busy to do all the work of evangelism alone. It was obvious that a coordinator could be a valuable asset to the pastor and the church.

Therefore, Charles Beach and Leonard Albert wrote *The Lay Coordinator's Manual.* They said, "This is not an attempt to set up another church office but, within the framework of the local church, to charge at least one member with the task of making outreach soulwinning programs work successfully. It can also be used as a guidebook for any layman—anywhere—who desires to become involved in an interesting variety of soulwinning ministries." This manual was a blessing to all men in the denomination. It dealt with church growth, personal evangelism, follow-up evangelism, problem solving, altar counseling, lay apologetics, witnessing to Jews, dealing with the cults, hospital visitation, bus evangelism, jail ministry, street ministry, witnessing invasions and home Bible study cells.

Layman of the Century

Charles was named Layman of the Century at the General Assembly in Atlanta in August 1986. At the time of this award, the lay office was overseeing over 2,000 men's fellowships across the country. The office was continuing to act as an information and resource center for laypeople. They were still coordinating seminars and lecture series such as "Maximum Manhood."

Retirement From Department of Lay Ministries

Charles retired from the Department of Lay Ministries on September 15, 1999, because of health reasons. When he was honored in a chapel service at the Church of God headquarters, he said, "Let me remind you that the most important thing in life is the fulfillment of Jesus' own central mission: 'For the Son of Man is come to seek and to save that which was lost' (Luke 19:10)." Dr. Beach relinquished official duties, but he continued to focus on personal evangelism and those who were hospitalized. Every day he visited the nursing homes in Cleveland and prayed with literally hundreds of people.

At his retirement somebody asked him how he would like to be thought of. Charles quickly responded, "A soul-winner. Soulwinning and personal evangelism is the only profession. There is not enough personal evangelism going on. Anyone who knows how to witness should teach it."

Charles put over 300,000 miles on his Rambler. Mitch Maloney says, "I wish we could put that Rambler on a pole in front of headquarters and put a bronzed pair of his hushpuppy shoes in the archives of the church."

9

THE PRAYER LIFE OF GOD'S SOLDIER

One of the most exciting aspects was Charles' life of prayer. He led the Lee College student body in prayer at chapel services. The students turned to him for prayer for serious problems in their lives. His wife said that it was not unusual to find him praying from midnight until 3:00 in the morning. "It takes me three hours a day of prayer to get through my prayer list," he would say. However, he did admit that it took him 30 years of disciplined development to reach this plateau of prayer life.

He Had Been Healed

Charles was a great believer in the power of prayer. When he prayed, he expected results. While teaching at Lee College, he had a severe stomach ulcer that plagued him for over two years. The Sunday school superintendent of Mount Olive sensed one night that he would be healed. Lois's father, Reverend J.L. Underwood, then pastor of the Mount Olive Church of God in Cleveland, prayed for him and he was healed instantly. "I felt the warmth of the Holy Spirit penetrate my body," Charles told his wife. "It felt like lightning had gone through me." He was never bothered again by ulcers.

Until the end of his life, Charles had an unceasing daily prayer life in which he prayed over lists of hundreds of names. He prayed for sinners, the sick, cultists, friends, family, church leaders, colleagues, students, bus children, ministers, lay leaders and his pastor.

Director of Prayerborne

Charles had gone back to Lee College as Christian service director when Ray H. Hughes became president of the college again in 1982. He remained there until 1988. Again God used him and students loved him, but his burden was for the entire church.

When Raymond Crowley was general overseer, he initiated a prayer commission to promote prayer in the church. One of the things he and the prayer commission set in operation was Prayerborne, a prayer army of retired ministers and other seniors who came together to pray for the church. They had hoped that this idea would catch on, and states and churches would also begin using their retired ministers to pray for the church.

When they began looking for the director, they felt that Charles was the man. They needed someone who was a leader, someone who had a powerful prayer life of his own. The Department of Evangelism and Home Missions asked that Prayerborne be placed under their leadership to help strengthen SAFE (Senior Adult Fellowship Endeavor).

This made Charles very happy—to be back on staff in the Evangelism Department again.

Every Wednesday the group met in the chapel of the headquarters building. Charles always passed out a sheet listing the needs for the group to pray about. He began the meeting with an expression of appreciation for their being there to pray for the church. They shared prayer requests, then he released them to pray in their own way. These were, after all, veterans who had already established prayer patterns. Charles had his own unique prayer style. He would walk and pray. He would pace and pray. This position fit him like a glove.

On one occasion Al Taylor was hosting some leaders from another denomination. While giving them a tour of the International Offices, he suddenly heard a loud noise. "What's that?" he asked. "Oh, that's a prayer meeting of senior adults who pray for the church," he was told. When the tour was over, the visitors expressed their appreciation for the tour. Al said, "The thing with which they were most impressed was the prayer meeting in the chapel."

Charles always paid for many copies of materials he wanted to give to Prayerborne members, laity, students and those in his seminars, which he still conducted. When Leonard Albert saw how much personal money he was spending on copying, the Lay Department bought him a copier. "If you wear it out, we'll buy you a new one," Leonard said. "He did, and we did."

There was no place for his office except in the stock room. Leonard and the Lay Affairs Office offered him one of their offices for life. This became a great blessing again because of his great love for laymen and because of his prayer life. He prayed for the laymen of the Church of

God and the Department of Lay Affairs by the hours. He wrote the following guidelines for people who wanted to improve their prayer life.

How to Pray and What to Pray For

All Christians, ministers and laypeople are encouraged to "pray without ceasing" (1 Thessalonians 5:17) for a multiplicity of needs: for healing (James 5:15), for freedom from temptation (Matthew 6:11), for forgiveness of sins (Luke 11:4; Acts 8:22), and for deliverance from the Evil One (Matthew 6:13).

Since Jesus began the Lord's Prayer with praise ("Our Father . . . Hallowed be thy name" [Luke 11:2]); since the persecuted disciples began their prayer with worship and praise ("Lord, thou *art* God; which hast made heaven, and earth, and the sea, and all that in them is" [Acts 4:24]); and since the leper who was cleansed (Matthew 8:2, 3), the ruler whose daughter was raised from the dead (Matthew 9:18, 25), and the demoniac who was delivered (Mark 5:6, 8, 13) all began their petitions with worship and praise, we have good and successful examples to follow for the opening of our own daily prayers:

"Lord, You are God: 'Before You there was no God formed, neither shall there be after You.' You made all things, 'and without You there was not anything made that was made.' 'All things were created by You, and for You'— the earth, the moon, the planets, the sun, the galaxies, the entire universe—'and You are before all things, and by You all things consist.' And You have all power and all authority 'in heaven and in earth.' Praise Your mighty,

Your high, and Your holy name" (see Isaiah 43:10; John 1:3; Colossians 1:16, 17).

What to Pray For: Family, Friends and Relatives

Samuel heavily emphasized the seriousness of our praying for our close friends and loved ones: "Moreover as for me [Samuel], God forbid that I should sin against the Lord in ceasing to pray for you [the Israelites, his friends, and family]" (1 Samuel 12:23).

How to Pray: "Jehovah God—Father, Son, and Holy Ghost—I lift up (names of family members and friends) and lay them on Your altar. I plead Your Holy Spirit's spiritual hedge of protection—in the name of Jesus, through the blood of Jesus, through the power of the Holy Ghost, and because of Your love, and His stripes— around all of these loved ones (already named).

"I pray that You will give each of them an overwhelming touch of His stripes for healing and health, and overwhelming measure of Your wisdom to solve their problems, and overwhelming amount of Your grace to grow in, and an overwhelming outpouring of Your Holy Ghost to make them effective witnesses for You. I pray that You will make them effective witnesses, that You will open up opportunities for them to witness, that You will help them take advantage of their witnessing opportunities, that You will give them divine appointments for witnessing every day, and that You will send them forth as effective witnesses into the harvest."

Note: If I do not pray for my family and friends, then I do not really care about their eternal spiritual welfare.

135

What to Pray For: Laborers to Go Into the Harvest

One of the most forceful of the Lord's commands to pray dealt with soulwinners' going into the overripe harvest. "Then saith he unto his disciples [we are His disciples], The harvest truly is plenteous, but the labourers are few; Pray ye [His disciples] therefore the Lord of the harvest, that he will send forth labourers into his harvest" (Matthew 9:37, 38).

How to Pray: "I pray, Lord, that You will send forth effective laborers into the harvest from every effective Evangelical church, home, and institution in the world; from every effective Pentecostal and Charismatic church, home, and institution in the world; and from every effective Church of God church, home, institution, youth camp, camp meeting, retreat, assembly, Sunday school, branch of Sunday school, mission, class, school, institute, college, seminar, outreach, and conference in the world."

Note: If I do not love to see souls won to Christ, then I will not pray this important prayer.

What to Pray For: The Salvation of the Lost

The prayer of Jesus for the conversion of the backsliding Simon Peter sets a good example for us to intercede for the lost: "But I have prayed for thee, that thy faith fail not: and when thou art converted, strengthen thy brethren" (Luke 22:32).

How to Pray: Since it is the work of the Holy Spirit to convict or reprove the unsaved "world of sin, and of righteousness, and of judgment" (John 16:8), it is, therefore, proper to ask Him to accomplish this work in the hearts and lives of the lost: "I pray that You, Jehovah God the Holy Spirit, will give (him/ her/them) a conviction of sin, a desire to live righteously, and a fear of judgment—daily: morning, noon and night.

"I pray, Lord, that You will give (him/her/them) a clear insight into Your Biblical plan of salvation, a clear-cut insight into their errors in concept and doctrine, and a sufficiently overwhelming fear of ending up in hell that (he/she/they) will seek out Your plan of salvation in Your Word.

"I pray, Lord, that You will give (him/her/them) a great hunger for the Word, an insight into the Word, a desire to do Your will, an understanding of the truth, a strong desire to be saved, and an assurance of salvation when they become saved.

"I pray also, Lord, that You will grant (him/her/them) the faith to believe on Jesus, the grace to repent of and confess (his/her/their) sins, and the boldness to confess Christ before men (Acts 16:31; Luke 13:3; 1 John 1:9; and Romans 10:9, 10)."

Note: If I do not pray for the salvation of the unsaved, then I am not interested in the objective of Jesus "to seek and to save that which was lost."

What to Pray For: Readiness to Go in the Rapture

The Lord Jesus underscored the fact that it would take continual spiritual vigilance and prayer to escape the Tribulation: "Watch ye therefore, and pray always, that ye may be accounted worthy to escape [the Tribulation by leaving in the Rapture] all these things that shall come to pass, and to stand before the Son of man" (Luke 21:36).

How to Pray: "I pray, Lord, that You will place my entire family (name them) and me on Your altar; and I pray that You will keep us under the Blood, will keep our robes white, will keep us filled with Your Spirit, and will keep us looking for Your coming (Titus 2:13) and 'loving [Your] appearing' (2 Timothy 4:8). If You come today, tomorrow, tomorrow night, the next day, the next night, the next day, the next night . . . please, Lord, do not fail to take us with You, and please, Lord, do not leave us here for the Tribulation period."

Note: If I do not watch and pray in order "to escape" the Tribulation, then I am not really concerned about leaving in the Rapture.

What to Pray For: Pastors and All Spiritual Leaders

All Christians, laymen and ministers are particularly and, indeed, greatly obligated to hold their leaders up in prayer: their pastors, their district leaders, their state officials, their general officials, their local boards and councils, and their home-church teachers and ministers: "Remember them which have rule over you, who have spoken unto you the word of God" (Hebrews 13:7).

How to Pray: (For the first part of this prayer, use essentially the same as that for friends and family.) "Lord, I pray for all of their soulwinning, discipling and equipping programs, especially for those of the Executive Committee, of the Executive Council, of the department heads, of the Lay Ministries Office, of all of the colleges and institutes around the world, of the local church ministers and leaders, of the state leaders, and of all the national and territorial officials on the mission fields all over the world. Lord, give them souls for their hire!

"I pray, Lord, for all of the problems—spiritual, financial, personal, administrative—that are met and faced by all of these church leaders. I lift these problems up, Lord, and place them on Your altar; and I pray, Almighty God, that You will come against the enemy of these problems being resolved and that You, Jehovah God—Father, Son, and Holy Spirit—will cause all of these multitudes of problems to be resolved in a manner which will cause Your church to grow, and to be resolved in a way that will give the right sense of spiritual direction to every adherent of this church throughout the world."

Note: If I have no spiritual vision for the future direction of my church—on both the local and national levels—then I will not pray for its leadership.

What to Pray For: The Peace of Jerusalem and the Jews

One group of people who are seldom mentioned in prayer requests are the Jews. However, God not only directs us to pray for them but promises prosperity to those who love the Jews enough to obey this command ("Pray for the peace of Jerusalem: they shall prosper that love thee" [Psalm 122:6]) and pronounces a blessing upon those who "bless thee"—the Jew—and a "curse" upon "him that curseth thee" (Genesis 12:3).

How to Pray: "I pray, Lord, that You will put Your hedge of protection around Your city, Jerusalem, and around all of its inhabitants and visitors. I pray that You will make that city and its people—especially the Jews—peaceful, safe, harmonious and warless.

"I lift up all of the Jews, Israelis and Hebrews around the world, Lord, and lay them on Your altar; and I pray . . . (use essentially here the prayer of salvation).

"I pray also, Father, that You will give every Jew, Israeli and Hebrew around the world an understanding of and an insight into the messiahship of Jesus of Nazareth, into Daniel 9, Isaiah 53, the deity of Christ, the divinity of Christ, the Yahwehness of Christ, the Jehovahness of Christ, the Godness of Christ, the Godship of Christ, the Godhood of Christ, the Godhead of Christ, the deity and personality of the Holy Spirit, the Trinity, the bodily resurrection of Christ, the physical return of Christ in the air at the end of the Tribulation, and eternal punishment for the unsaved."

Note: If I do not pray for the Israelis and Jerusalem, then I do not really love the Jews.

How to Receive Answers to Prayer

Ask unselfishly: "Ye have not, because ye ask not. Ye ask, and receive not, because ye ask amiss, that ye may consume it upon your lusts" (James 4:2, 3).

Ask, seek and knock with perseverance: "Ask, and it shall be given you; seek, and ye shall find; knock and it shall be opened unto you" (Matthew 7:7).

Pray continuously, without giving in to discouragement: "Men ought always to pray, and not to faint" (Luke 18:1).

Remain in Christ and in His Word: "If ye abide in me, and my words abide in you, ye shall ask what ye will, and it shall be done unto you" (John 15:7).

Live a righteous life and pray fervently: "The effectual fervent prayer of a righteous man availeth much" (James 5:16).

Ask according to His will: "And this is the confidence that we have in him, that , if we ask any thing according to his will, he heareth us: And if we know that he hear us, whatsoever we ask, we know that we have the petitions that we desired of him" (1 John 5:14, 15).

Express thankfulness: "Be careful for nothing; but in every thing by prayer and supplication with thanksgiving let your requests be made known unto God" (Philippians 4:6).

Pray in the Spirit: "Praying always with all prayer and supplication in the Spirit" (Ephesians 6:18). "Likewise the Spirit also helpeth our infirmities: for we know not what we should pray for as we ought: but the Spirit itself maketh intercession for us with groanings which cannot be uttered. And he that searcheth the hearts knoweth what *is* the mind of the Spirit, because he maketh intercession for the saints according to the will of God" (Romans 8:26, 27).

Know that the Lord, your best problem solver, desires to hear—in prayers—every single care, problem, hurt, pain, fear, adversity, failure, hardship, pressure, rejection, worry, anxiety, burden, grief, sorrow, heartache and trouble that you may possibly experience. "Casting all [*all, all, all, all*] your care upon him; for he careth for you (1 Peter 5:7).

141

10

FAMILY LIFE

Family life always remained the greatest priority for Charles Beach. Lois Underwood Beach was the most important person in his life. Their 5 p.m. dinner dates were always the highlight of his day. He often told people how lucky he was to have such a beautiful and brilliant wife.

Charles took great pride in Lois' accomplishments. He was thrilled when she was given an honorary doctor's degree in May 1981, which had been initiated by a group of senior science majors. He proudly said, "I'm the husband of a doctor." Then he was elated beyond words when on December 9, 1989, Lee named the science building "Lois Underwood Beach Science Building."

Humor was also a part of their family life. He was always teasing Lois. When he was on trips or invasions, he always called home regularly. He would greet Lois with statements like, "Lois, are you sober yet?" He loved to hear her laugh.

Humor

Charles Beach enjoyed bringing laughter and relaxation to people. He first started dressing and performing like Charley Weaver, a popular comedian of the 1950s, for the students and faculty of Lee College for banquets and special occasions. Then he was asked to speak to various groups throughout the denomination. The amazing thing was that when he was dressed in costume, he looked just like Charley Weaver.

The audience loved his "Letters from Mamma" performances. He wrote many of his own, but he also used Charley Weaver's *Letters From Mamma,* by Cliff Arquette.

His Goals

Charles had always set high goals and standards for himself; therefore, he set high goals and standards for his family. He never expected anything from others that he did not first expect from himself. Therefore, he gave them goals to aim toward.

The family financial situation was difficult when their only daughter, Sharlinda, was young. Nevertheless, he would take her to Coopers Bookstore. He sat on the floor, put Sharlinda in his lap and read entire books to her. The manager loved it.

Charles often took Sharlinda to the park and on long walks to look at the gardens in town. Sometimes they would walk to downtown Cleveland for a hamburger at the Spot (a small soda shop), or go to a local ice cream parlor for an ice cream cone.

PFC students were always in the Beach's home. Sharlinda picked up on the fact that every Christian should be a witness. As a young elementary school student, she would go to school and ask the other children if they were saved. If they said "No," she would tell them they were going to hell. The kids told the principal, Mr. Wilson. His reply was, "Leave Sharlinda alone. She has a story to tell."

Helping the Needy

People who had needs were always knocking on their door. One Saturday morning they heard a knock. It was a man who had just gotten out of jail. Lois went to get her husband. The man said, "Beach, while I was in jail, you said that if a man has two coats and someone asks for one, he should give him one. Do you have two coats?" Charles said, "Yes," and offered him the only two coats he had. Lois and Sharlinda were in the back room listening to every word. Sharlinda said, "I bet he takes the best one." Sure enough, the man reached out and took the best coat and started to leave. Charles said, "Wait a minute. I am giving you this coat in the name of the Lord. Come in and let's pray." The prayer lasted 30 minutes, but the man became a soulwinner and won many to Christ in Cleveland—particularly in the jails.

Almost every week somebody in need was at their door. They needed money, food or clothing. God helped the Beaches to be able to share what they had, and Charles always used it as an opportunity to witness. Many times they emptied their entire pantry and gave what they had to those in need. There were no discussions or debates. It was the feeling of both Lois and Charles that the hungry had to be fed and they were often the ones God called upon to do it.

On one occasion Charles was out of town. Lois woke up and realized that someone had spent the night on her back porch. She went outside and saw the man. "Mr. Beach led me to the Lord in jail. I knew it would be all right to sleep on his porch," he said. Lois did not want a strange man sleeping on her porch with Charles out of town, so she gave him some money for a motel and food and sent him on his way.

His Pride and Joy

Charles and Lois are very proud of their only daughter, Sharlinda Beach Turner, who is a medical doctor. Some of Sharlinda's earliest memories are of visiting with her father in homes, hospitals, nursing homes and jails to share with others the love of God. Those were always special memories.

When Sharlinda was in labor with her first child, a nurse came out and told them the baby had arrived, but she would not tell then what it was. She said the doctor wanted to tell the family. Lois followed her toward the area and looked around to find that Charles was not with them. She went to look for him down the hall and found him in an area by the window. She said, "Honey, we have waited all night for this occurrence and then you disappear. Where in the world have you been?" He said, "I went to pray one more time for a little girl." Lois said, "Aren't you a little late?" His response was, "No, I wanted to remind God of all my prayers I had prayed for years for a little girl."

His Granddaughters

God answered his prayers and gave them two granddaughters, Cindy and Christa, who brought him and Lois great joy.

Cindy was the first granddaughter. Early in life she aspired to be a writer. This was the thrill of Charles Beach's life. He proofed her papers for school and told her over and over that she could be a writer. He instilled confidence in her. Cindy is now majoring in journalism.

He began taking Cindy to nursing homes with him when she was very young. They spent many Sunday afternoons at the nursing homes together. It was a way for them to be together. Cindy says, "I remember how the people he visited just beamed in his presence because his visits meant so much to them."

He continued doing some of the same things for his granddaughters he had done for Sharlinda. He took them to the same park to play, to a local pizza restaurant that had costumed characters and video games. He attended their performances and award ceremonies.

Christa speaks today about some of the principles her grandfather instilled into her. She writes, "He put his pride aside to help others. He taught me it was better to give than to receive. He told me people really were good and most intentions were meant well."

He shared war stories with his granddaughters few people ever heard. He only shared those touching moments with those to whom he was closest.

Christa was like a little soldier to him, because she never showed her emotions in public. He often said she was just like him. Those of us who know him best question that, because he did show his deep feelings in public. We loved him for it!

Many times in seminars Charles taught on prayer. He would pass out his tract on "How to Pray and What to Pray For." Then he would teasingly say, "I pray for my church; then I pray for my granddaughters; I pray for my country; then I pray for my granddaughters. I pray for my church's leaders. Then I pray for my granddaughters. I pray for my country's leaders. Then I pray for my granddaughters. Why? Because I will not be here when they are older, and the devil will try to affect them one way or another. So, I am banking my prayers up in heaven for them now."

He always said, "My granddaughters are like the little prince in the French classic *Le Petit Prince*, by Antoine de Saint-Exupery. They 'sunshine' the house."

On one occasion the entire family went to England. Cindy was about 6 years old. They went to the Tower of London. Charles was always terrified by heights. But Lois looked around, and Charles and Cindy were climbing the stairs to the top of the tower. There were a lot of stairs to climb, but he made the effort for his granddaughter. At the top, he bought her a set of "crown jewels." This was a memorable time for her and the family.

His Passion

He loved his country and was proud of the flag he fought under. He had told his granddaughters about being in the war. "I'd do it again for my family and for my country," he'd say.

Charles Beach enjoyed big and small celebrations. Two of the family's most treasured family memories were spending the turn of the millennium together at Walt Disney World and celebrating his 78th birthday before his death in November 2000.

He had written in the *Church of God Evangel* (December 26, 1983): "If you ask me what I want on my tombstone I'd say, 'He loved his family and spent some time in the harvest.'" Someone suggested it would be better to say, "He loved his family and had a passion for the harvest."

11

GROWING OLDER FRUITFULLY

To grow old fruitfully was the decision of this great soldier of the Cross. He wrote in the December 1983 *Church of God Evangel*:

I have found that growing old gracefully requires careful attention to at least four different areas of one's active life:

1. His spiritual life
2. His physical life
3. His mental life
4. His social life

My own personal philosophy concerning my spiritual life is that I must keep active—very active—in my worship, in my prayer, in my giving, and especially in my daily witnessing for Christ.

Spending Time in Writing to Leave a Legacy

Much of the latter years of Charles' life were spent in writing. There were some things he felt the Church of God needed that he had not had time to write. After spending at least three hours in prayer every day and witnessing several hours, the rest of his time was given to writing. Part Two of this book is one of the most cogent works available on the Holy Spirit Baptism.

Encouraging Seniors to Witness in Nursing Homes

Charles suggested that older people could witness in nursing homes. He said, "The residents in Life Care Centers for the elderly are often abandoned by their families, forsaken by an uncaring society, and neglected by a worldly and lukewarm church. This is an ideal situation for senior citizens who desire to win or encourage souls for Christ."

Charles began daily visitation to an elderly, lifelong Jehovah's Witness in the Garden Terrace Nursing Home. Often they discussed her life and the rearing of her children—subjects dear to her heart. At other times her conversation focused on the Bible—particularly on the subject of eternal punishment in the lake of fire. The fear of this reality concerned her greatly. Each time she brought up the subject, Charles would read to her from her own *New World Translation*, a Watchtower version of the Bible: "And they (including two human beings who had been in the lake of fire for a thousand years without being annihilated) will be tormented day and night forever and ever" (Revelation 20:10). Ultimately she accepted the fact that the unsaved faced an eternal hell. She then accepted Christ a few days before she passed away. For Charles, the joy of snatching another soul out of the lake of fire was a tremendous blessing. He was blessed to know that he was being used of the Lord to fulfill his primary objective at an age when many were retiring.

Hospital Visitation for Senior Adults

Many people in both hospitals and nursing homes called Charles Beach their pastor. Though he never held ministerial license, he pastored hurting people who were sick and lonely and had no one to be there for them.

Hospital visitation on a daily basis was another spiritually fruitful ministry for Charles. He was able to get into almost any room in the hospital. He knew how to develop relationships with the hospital personnel. He often brought ice cream to the nurses on duty. That was just another sign of his giving nature.

A born-again Baptist nurse directed him to the room of a cancer patient who was unsaved and filled with fear. Charles visited him on three successive evenings before he felt he had earned the right to present the gospel. He prayed the sinner's prayer but showed little evidence of the new birth. About a month later because of his worsening condition, he was readmitted to the hospital. This time, however, he showed evidence of a spiritual change. Just to make sure, Charles asked him to pray the sinner's prayer with him one more time. He did pray and Charles left his room that night feeling great victory. The next morning, his newborn Christian friend left this life to spend eternity with Jesus. Charles commented, "Successful soul-winning experiences such as this, which occur fairly frequently in my hospital visitation, make my aging experience one of spiritual delight."

Never Lost the Vision of Winning the Lost

His involvement in other witnessing ministries included jail visitation, house-to-house visitation, and visiting in the homes of shut-ins.

When he was 75 years old, this legendary lay witness was given a 75th birthday celebration and ceremony. In his response to the reception, Beach told of that very day leading a 70-year-old woman, who had never been saved before, in the sinner's prayer. Which was the highlight of his day—the reception with church leaders and college professors or the winning of that 70-year-old woman to the Lord? Without any doubt, the winning of the lost was more important to him than anything else in this world. Marcus Hand wrote: "Even in responding to well-deserved accolades, he managed to motivate others to want to witness for Christ."

Giving Continued to Be a Priority

Giving was always a vital part of Charles' life. He gave when he did not have it to give. In one of the most financially difficult periods of his life, he raised his tithing, giving one percent extra per year for several years, which resulted in great material and spiritual blessings. In his later years, he had the assurance that he had pleased the Lord in his finances.

Exercise and Good Nutrition

Watching so many people who were chair-bound in nursing homes, Charles determined to exercise regularly. He believed that a lot of people were no longer ambulatory simply because they sat down and refused to walk or exercise. He swam two or three times a week at a local spa.

He became very health-conscious in his senior years, eating nutritious, well-balanced meals that included vegetables, enriched or whole-grain cereals, a lot of skim milk and lean meats. He avoided foods with saturated fats.

Social Life Was Important

Charles said his social needs were met in two ways—through fellowship with teaching colleagues and with ministering students, and through a great family life. He wrote the following Senior Adult Manifesto.

I am a Church of God senior adult. As a Church of God senior adult, I have, first of all, a solemn obligation to support my church and to back my pastor in every soul-winning endeavor he undertakes (1 Corinthians 4:2).

As a Church of God senior adult, I have a solemn obligation to pray for my pastor-shepherd every day (1 Timothy 2:1, 2).

As a Church of God senior adult, I have a solemn obligation to back my pastor with my tithes and offerings. If I do not, I am robbing God (Malachi 3:8-10; Matthew 23:23).

As a Church of God senior adult, I have an obligation to let my pastor know I love and appreciate him and his ministry (1 Thessalonians 5:12, 13).

As a Church of God senior adult, I have an obligation to offer to assist my pastor in his visitation programs in hospitals, nursing homes and elderly housing projects (Acts 5:42; Matthew 25:34-46).

As a Church of God senior adult, I have an obligation to help my pastor in the bus ministry and in the inception of branch Sunday schools (Luke 14:21-23).

As a Church of God senior adult, I have an obligation to help my pastor in his house-to-house witnessing program (Acts 20:20).

If I, a Church of God senior adult, do not fulfill these obligations, if I do not witness for Christ, then "I am a hearer of the Word and not a doer, deceiving myself" (see James 1:22).

If I, a Church of God senior adult, do not witness for Christ, then my faith, having no works, being alone, is absolutely dead (James 2:17).

If I, a Church of God senior adult, fail to witness for Christ, it is because I am filled with my own ways and am therefore a backslider in heart (Proverbs 14:14; James 4:17).

If I, a Church of God senior adult, fail to witness to the poor lost souls of this world, whom I should love, then I have lost my first love and the Lord has somewhat against me (Revelation 2:4).

If I, a Church of God senior adult, fail to witness for Christ and do not the works of the Lord, then my "heart goeth after covetousness" while I show love only with my lips (Ezekiel 33:30-33).

If I, a Church of God senior adult, fail to witness for Christ and fail to save others "with fear, pulling them out of the fire," then I help to usher these same precious souls into an eternal, everlasting, non-ending, tormenting hell (Jude 23).

But I cannot, I must not fail. As a Church of God senior adult in these last days just before the imminent return of the Lord, I cannot afford to become at ease in Zion (Amos 6:1).

Many, many people in this country are satisfied because they are free from tyranny and oppression. Many, many Christians are satisfied because they are free from the penalty of sin.

But may God grant that I, as a Church of God senior adult Christian, never ever be satisfied until I can say, as Paul said, "I am free and pure from the blood of all men" (Acts 20:26).

12

FROM HERE
TO ETERNITY

In Charles' later years, he developed Alzheimer's disease, but this did not stop him. When this condition was just originating, he made a trip alone to Salt Lake City. Again he witnessed to hundreds.

Lois kept life going just as it had always been. She responded to letters he received. Beth Hamon, the daughter of Randy and Kathy Hamon, sent him a notice of her graduation in the year 2000. Lois sent a letter back: "Beth, Charles always loved you. If he saw you today, he may not know who you are, but he would want you to have a graduation gift from him. So I am sending you this money in honor of him."

As the disease developed, Lois took him to the nursing home every day to witness to people there. The week before he died, he laid his hands on an older lady in the nursing home and prayed, "Oh, God! Please help this lady. She just can't think like she used to. It is such a bother to her. She wants to be able to think right again. Please help her to think clearly." Lois stood there with tears streaming down her face. These were his own feelings about himself.

He Built Memories

One week before Charles went to be with the Lord, he and Lois were in a restaurant in Cleveland. A young woman walked up to the table and said, "Charles, you don't remember me. When I was a little girl (I am now 30), you came every Sunday morning in your station wagon and took me, along with other children, to North Cleveland to Sunday school. I am a Christian today because of that."

That same week an older man came to them in another restaurant. He said, "My father was in ICU at Bradley Memorial Hospital, and you prayed with him. You came back out and sat with us in the waiting room most of the night. We did not have a church or pastor, so you conducted the funeral. You told us at the funeral that my father accepted the Lord when you prayed with him in ICU, and you were confident that he was in heaven."

Study of the Holy Spirit

The last few years of Charles Beach's life, he spent hundreds of hours studying and researching the Holy Spirit. He wanted to write something that would live after him about the power of the Holy Spirit. After all, his entire life was the acts of the Holy Spirit. He would spend hours studying one verse in all the various languages and translations. He wanted even the commas and brackets perfect. He paid $30 a page to get it typed the way he wanted.

One day he said to Lois, "I have this material done; but it doesn't look like I'm going to get it published. I'm running out of time. You'll have to do it for me. I want people to know about the purpose of the Holy Spirit."

Still Praying for Others

Charles developed pneumonia and became critically ill. The last few nights of his life his daughter, Dr. Sharlinda Turner, stayed with him at night so her mother could get some rest. Sharlinda was so moved when he would lie there all night, praying in all five of the languages he spoke. He would pray in English, then Spanish, then French, then German and then Russian. He prayed for his family, for the church, for the leaders of the church, for the leaders of the country, for the Jews and the return of the Jews. He called the names of hundreds of people. He would pray for people around the world—even the descendants of missionaries such as the late great Herman Lauster, who had spent time in a concentration camp.

His Homegoing

When he was in the hospital, Lois was attempting to show him how to breathe in the mask so he could get more oxygen. He looked at her and laughed and said, "You are funny. I love you." Then he was taken to ICU and never spoke again.

He went to be with the Lord on November 17, 2000. Leonard Albert and Mitch Maloney were with him to the end. They both presided at the funeral.

His was a military funeral. His nephew, Chaplain Melvin H. Underwood, LCDR, U.S. Navy, presided over the cemetery service. The American Legion Honor Guard gave the gun salute, played taps and presented the flag to his wife. Charles was a proud sailor to the end.

After the funeral, Lois took her granddaughter Cindy with her to give some of the flowers she had been sent to various nursing homes where Charles visited. Receptionists wept. They fondly remembered the man who cared so much about the people there.

God, we ask that You give the rest of us a double portion of the anointing of Charles Beach in winning the lost. Help us to get our hands into the harvest.

When Moses died, God told Joshua, "Moses my servant is dead; now therefore arise, go over this Jordan, thou, and all this people, unto the land which I do give to them, even to the children of Israel. Every place that the sole of your foot shall tread upon, that have I given unto you" (Joshua 1:2, 3). If Charles Beach could speak from the bannisters of heaven to you today, he would say, "Go! Go! Go! Witness on the street corners. Witness in the homes. Witness at the gas stations. Witness in the restaurants. Witness on the airplanes. Witness to the rich. Witness to the poor. Witness to the white. Witness to the black. Witness to the Orientals. Witness everywhere you go."

If Charles could talk with you personally today, he would tell you that after receiving the Holy Spirit, you receive *dunamis,* which is the miracle-working power of God. He would tell you that after you receive the Holy

Spirit, you receive the "ability of God" to witness in Jerusalem, in Judea, in Samaria, and even to the uttermost parts of the world. He would tell you that when you receive the Holy Spirit you receive the Comforter or *Parakletos*, the One called alongside to help.

Charles Beach allowed the Holy Spirit to use him to bring others to Christ. May there be a transference of his spirit to us today. When we receive the spirit of our mentor, we are enabled to do what our mentor did to a degree.

After Elijah threw his mantle upon Elisha, recognition of destiny was awakened in Elisha. With Charles Beach's passing into heaven, a sense of destiny must be awakened in us. After reading this book, may the mantle of Charles Beach fall upon you! May you have a double-portion anointing. Jesus said, "Greater works than these that I do shall you do, because I go to my Father" (see John 14:12). May you do greater works than Charles did, because he went to be with the Father.

⩔ PART TWO ⩔

THE
HOLY SPIRIT

WITNESSING AND THE HOLY SPIRIT

As Leonard Albert said, "These are thoughts from a man who lived by the Spirit. During his entire Christian life, Charles Beach had a desire to help more individuals receive more of the Spirit of God."

Charles began this study in 1945 after accepting salvation on board a troop ship returning home from World War II. This study spanned more than 50 years, and the scriptures were reviewed in many languages. His last comment in reference to this material was, "My time is running out. I want to get this published. I feel that it will help someone." By the request of Charles Beach, this section of the book is just as he wrote it with a few exceptions of some "House" rules common to Christian publishing.

POWER TO WITNESS FOR CHRIST

"And with great power gave the apostles witness of the resurrection of the Lord Jesus" (Acts 4:33).

The primary objective of the Lord Jesus Christ in coming to this earth was "to seek and to save that which was lost" (Luke 19:10). The purpose of the baptism in the Holy Ghost is to endue the born-again, Spirit-begotten believer in Christ with greater spiritual power, in order that he may be more dynamic—and thus a more effective—witness and soulwinner for the Lord to help fulfill that primary objective: "But ye shall receive power, after that the Holy Ghost is come upon you: and ye shall be witnesses unto me . . . unto the uttermost part of the earth" (Acts 1:8).

Evidence of Powerful Witnessing

This powerful, bold witnessing was exampled by Christ's disciples on and after the Day of Pentecost: "And they were all filled with the Holy Ghost, and they spake the word of God with boldness" (Acts 4:31). "And with great power gave the apostles witness of the resurrection of the Lord Jesus: and great grace was upon them all" (v. 33).

The apostle Peter, who was baptized in the Holy Spirit on the Day of Pentecost and who preached to and won thousands (2:41) on that same day, nevertheless witnessed to, and healed (through Christ), and won the lame man "at the gate . . . which is called Beautiful" (3:1-11). Later, "filled with the Holy Ghost" (4:8), the same apostle Peter, who, with John, had been arrested for preaching the resurrection through Christ (vv. 2, 3), boldly testified to the Jewish "rulers, and elders, and scribes" (v. 5) that "neither is there salvation in any other: for there is none other name under heaven given among men, whereby we must be saved" (v. 12).

When Peter and John were released by the Jewish leaders, they returned to the other disciples and reported the threats. Christians began to praise and magnify God, and "And when they had prayed, the place was shaken where they were assembled together; and they [the same disciples who had been baptized in the Holy Ghost on the Day of Pentecost] were all filled with the Holy Ghost [shouting that a Christian can be baptized in the Spirit and then, later, filled with God's Holy Spirit], and they spake the word of God with boldness" (v. 31; see also vv. 23-31).

What was the major purpose of their being filled again with God's Holy Ghost? "And with great power gave the apostles witness of the resurrection of the Lord Jesus" (v. 33).

One of those disciples who witnessed "with great power" was Stephen. "Stephen, a man full of . . . the Holy Ghost" (6:5), a layman who was "full of faith and power" (v. 8), testified boldly to the Sanhedrin: "Ye have now been the betrayers and murderers" of the "Just One" (7:52). And it cost Stephen his life.

But the Lord Jesus, of whom it is said over 20 times in the Bible that He is seated "at the right hand of the throne of God" (Hebrews 12:2), stood up on this occasion to honor His martyred lay witness and to welcome Stephen home to heaven—for eternity: "But he [Stephen], being full of the Holy Ghost, looked up steadfastly into heaven, and saw the glory of God, and Jesus standing on the right hand of God [Stephen, full of the Holy Ghost (called God in Acts 5:3, 4), saw Jesus (called God in Hebrews 1:8) at God's right hand (good Trinitarian theology). . . . And he kneeled down, and cried with a loud voice, Lord, lay not this sin to their charge" (Acts 7:55, 60).

169

The Enhanced Effectiveness of the Spirit-filled Evangelical Witness

The case of Apollos—the Alexandrian Jew, who was "an eloquent man, and mighty in the scriptures . . . instructed in the way of the Lord; and . . . fervent in the spirit [he was already "born of . . . the Spirit" (John 3:5)], [and who] spake and taught diligently the things of the Lord, knowing only [repeat: 'only'] the baptism of John" (Acts 18:24, 25)—shows that even a very talented, very bold Evangelical worker for Christ can improve the effectiveness of his witnessing—making it even more powerful, mightier and bolder—when he is baptized in the Holy Ghost.

Apollos, who spoke "boldly [but only?] in the synagogue" (v. 26), knew, as already indicated, "only the baptism of John" (v. 25). His was the same spiritual state as that of the longtime Ephesian disciples in the next chapter (19:3) for whom Paul prayed to receive the Spirit baptism: "And when Paul had laid his hands upon them, the Holy Ghost came on them; and they spake with tongues, and prophesied" (v. 6).

Now Apollos, according to *The Pulpit Commentary* (XVIII, 107), "had not got beyond the 'baptism of John,' and knew little of the 'baptism of the Holy Ghost.'" And *Matthew Henry's Commentary* (VI, 241) states specifically that "he was not baptized with the Holy Ghost, as the disciples were at the day of Pentecost." But Apollos, "was, bearing already 'much fruit'"

(*The Pulpit Commentary* XVIII, 1073) at the time that he met some itinerant tentmaker-evangelists, Aquila and his wife, Priscilla, who, having traveled with and, most likely, learned from Paul (18:18, 19), "took him [Apollos] unto them, and expounded unto him the way of God more perfectly" (v. 26). And *The Pulpit Commentary* notes further that they "perceiving that his knowledge was imperfect", "instructed fulness of the truth of the gospel" (XVIII, 93), "telling him the latest and the best" (XVIII, 107).

Did their explanation include instructions on the baptism in the Holy Ghost? The commentator's notes in *Dake's Annotated Reference Bible* say that it did: "*John's disciples* could receive baptism in water, but *Christ's disciples* the baptism in the Holy Spirit, hence the inquiry of Paul ["Have ye received the Holy Ghost since ye believed?" (19:2)]. This was part of the gospel Apollos learned [from Aquila and Priscilla] in Acts 18:26" (*Dake's Annotated Reference Bible*, p. 146 of the New Testament, left column, note c).

And Apollos's obviously enhanced witnessing capabilities support the contention of the commentator: "For he [Apollos, after Aquila and Priscilla had "expounded unto him the way of God more perfectly"] mightily [powerfully: "ye shall receive power, after that the Holy Ghost is come upon you: and ye shall be witnesses unto me" (Acts 1:8); "and they were all filled with the Holy Ghost. . . . And with great power gave the apostles witness of the resurrection" (4:31, 33)] convinced the Jews, and that [that what?] (that "mightily [convincing] the Jews") publicly, showing by the scriptures that Jesus was Christ" (18:28).

Apollos was a very talented, very learned, very spiritual, very diligent Evangelical preacher, teacher and witness who was born of the Spirit (John 3:3, 5) and who therefore had received the power of sonship mentioned study session with Aquila and Priscilla (Acts 18:26), he became a more powerful Pentecostal witness who "mightily [powerfully] convinced the Jews, *and that* publickly [no longer just inside the safe walls of the synagogue?], shewing by the scriptures that Jesus was Christ" (v. 28). He had gone from possessing just "the power of sonship" (the birth of the Spirit, John 1:12, 13; 3:3, 5) to possessing "the power to witness" (the baptism in the Spirit, Acts 1:8) as well. The example of Apollos shows that the baptism in the Holy Ghost improves, enhances and makes more effective the work of any and every witness for Christ, regardless of his or her previous talents.

Spirit Baptism Promised to All Flesh

The general outpouring of the Holy Spirit, which first occurred in the New Testament on the Day of Pentecost, was promised, not just to a few apostles and leaders, but to "all people" (Acts 2:17, *NIV*) or "all flesh" (KJV), both men and women, young and old, apostles, disciples and all believers (John 7:37-39), without regard to age, rank or sex; thus preached Peter, quoting a prophecy from Joel 2:28, 29: "And it shall come to pass in the last days, saith God, I will pour out of my Spirit upon all flesh: and your sons and your daughters shall prophesy, and your young men shall see visions, and your old men shall dream dreams: And on my servants and on my handmaidens I will pour out in those days of my Spirit; and they shall prophesy" (Acts 2:17, 18).

In the same sermon (vv. 38, 39) the apostle Peter stated that "gift of the Holy Ghost" was for "every one of you"—the thousands of Jews who heard him that day—and for "your children," the born, and the unborn. The "promise" was "to all . . . [emphasis on "all," all down through the centuries] *even* as many as the Lord our God shall call (even to those whom He is calling this year, this month, this week, even this very day and hour). "Then Peter said unto them, Repent, and be baptized every one of you in the name of Jesus Christ for [or, Greek *eis*, "as a result of" or "because of"] the remission of sins, and ye [the thousands who heard Peter that day] shall receive the gift of the Holy Ghost. For the promise is unto you, and to your children, and to all that are afar off, even as many as the Lord our God shall call" (vv. 38, 39).

NOTE: The conditions for receiving "the gift of the Holy Ghost" are: "[l] Repent, and [2] be baptized every one of you [3] in the name ["by the authority"] of Jesus Christ for [or, Greek *eis*, "as a result of" or "because of"] the remission of sins, and ye shall receive the gift of the Holy Ghost" (Acts 2:38). The first condition was to repent. The act of repentance was, and is, absolutely necessary as a prerequisite to salvation according to the Lord Jesus Christ, who was literally "God with us" (Matthew 1:23) and who, therefore, could not lie (Titus 1:2; Hebrews 6:18): "I tell you, Nay: but, except ye repent [change your attitude toward and your love for sin and forsake it], ye shall all likewise perish" (Luke 13:3).

The adherents to the doctrine that water baptism actually saves souls from hell must never forget or omit this extremely important commandment to repent of and forsake one's sins. The scripture that is used to support the teaching that water baptism saves souls, 1 Peter 3:21, indicates clearly that baptism does not put away the "filth of the flesh," that it does not remove the moral depravity or "works of the flesh" (see Galatians 5:19-21), that it is

173

simply "the answer of a good conscience toward God," and that this clean "conscience toward God" precedes baptism and is a result of faith in "the resurrection of Jesus Christ" (and it is this faith in the shed blood, death, entombment and resurrection of our Savior—of which water baptism is only a figure—that in reality saves the soul). "The like figure whereunto even baptism doth also now save us (not the putting away of the filth of the flesh, but the answer of a good conscience toward God,) by the resurrection of Jesus Christ" (1 Peter 3:21).

If water baptism does not redeem one and cleanse him of the filth and depravity of the flesh, what does?

- "Thou art worthy . . . for thou wast slain, and hast redeemed us to God by thy blood" (Revelation 5:9).

- "Forasmuch as ye know that ye were not redeemed with corruptible things . . . But with the precious blood of Christ" (1 Peter 1:18, 19).

- "Take heed . . . to feed the church of God, which he hath purchased with his own blood" (Acts 20:28).

- "Much more then, being now justified by his blood, we shall be saved from wrath through him" (Romans 5:9).

- "And, having made peace through the blood of his cross" (Colossians 1:20).

- "How much more shall the blood of Christ . . . purge your conscience ["the answer of a good conscience"] from dead works to serve the living God?" (Hebrews 9:14).

- "These are they which came out of great tribulation, and have washed their robes, and made them white in the blood of the Lamb" (Revelation 7:14).

- "But one of the soldiers with a spear pierced his side, and forthwith came there out blood and water" (John 19:34).

- "And they overcame him [the devil] by the blood of the Lamb" (Revelation 12:11).

- "Whom God hath set forth to be a propitiation through faith in his blood [not water], to declare his righteousness for the remission of sins that are past, through the forbearance of God" (Romans 3:25).

- "But if we walk in the light, as he is in the light, we have fellowship one with another, and the blood of Jesus Christ his Son [not water] cleanseth us from all [all, all, all, all] sin" (1 John 1:7).

The Baptism in the Holy Ghost Prophesied in the Old Testament

The outpouring of the Holy Ghost was prophesied by one of the minor prophets of the Old Testament, Joel, who excluded no one—man, woman or child—as a recipient of this great spiritual witnessing power: "And it shall come to pass afterward, *that* I will pour out of my spirit upon all flesh ["on all people," *NIV*]; and your sons and your daughters shall prophesy, your old men shall dream dreams, your young men shall see visions: And also upon the servants and upon the handmaids in those days will I pour out my spirit" (Joel 2:28, 29; see also Isaiah 28:11, 12). Note the fulfillment in Acts 2:16-21.

NOTE: Joel says that "your daughters shall prophesy." Paul defines prophesying—not always as telling the future but—as encouragement and edification of others: "But he that prophesieth speaketh unto men to edification, and exhortation, and comfort" (1 Corinthians 14:3). Paul gives proof that women did pray and preach in the early church: "But every woman that prayeth or prophesieth ["speaketh unto men to edification, and exhortation, and comfort"] with *her* head uncovered dishonoreth her head" (11:5).

The command by Paul three chapters later for women to "keep silence in the churches [congregations]" (14:34) had nothing to do with preaching or praying but with asking questions: "And if they will learn any thing, let them ask their husbands at home" (v. 35). "Philip the evangelist . . . had four daughters, virgins, which did prophesy" (Acts 21:8, 9). "And . . . help those women [Euodias and Syntyche] which labored with me in the gospel" (Philippians 4:2, 3). "I commend unto you Phebe our sister, which is a servant [deaconess, from Greek, *diakonon*] of the church which is at Cenchrea" (Romans 16:1; see also v. 2). "Salute Tryphena and Tryphosa, who labour in the Lord. Salute the beloved Persis, which laboured much in the Lord" (v. 12).

Paul does warn the woman, however, not "to usurp authority over the man" (1 Timothy 2:12); but he also gives to all men an extremely important commandment: "Husbands, love your wives, even as Christ also loved the church, and gave himself for it [now, that is really divine love, a lot of it]. . . . So ought men to love their wives as their own bodies. He that loveth his wife loveth himself. For no man ever yet hated his own flesh; but nourisheth and cherisheth it, even as the Lord the church" (Ephesians 5:25, 28, 29).

The Baptism in the Holy Ghost Prophesied in the New Testament

The baptism in the Holy Ghost was prophesied by John the Baptist: "I indeed have baptized you with water: but he shall baptize you with the Holy Ghost" (Mark 1:8; see also Matthew 3:11; Luke 3:16; John 1:33).

The outpouring of the Spirit of God was prophesied by the Lord Jesus Christ during the Feast of Tabernacles and was promised to every spiritually thirsty "man" or person: "In the last day, that great day of the feast, Jesus stood and cried, saying, If any man [no one excluded, no one excepted] thirst, let him come unto me, and drink. He that believeth on me [the promise is to every believer, to those that are already saved, to every born-again Christian], as the scripture hath said, out of his belly shall flow rivers of living water [limitless power to do His works (see John 14:12; Acts 1:8)]. "But this spake he of the Spirit, which they that believe on him should receive: for the Holy Ghost was not yet *given*; because that Jesus was not yet glorified" (John 7:37-39).

The gift of the Holy Ghost was prophesied and promised by Jesus as another Comforter who would "abide" with His followers forever: "And I will pray the Father, and he shall give you another Comforter [emphasis on "another," not the Son], that he may abide with you for ever; Even the Spirit of truth; whom the world cannot receive, because it seeth him not, neither knoweth him:

177

but ye know him; for he dwelleth with you, and shall be in you. I will not leave you comfortless: I will come to you [which He did several times (John 20:19, 26; Acts 1:3)]" (John 14:16-18).

NOTE: Jesus said that the Holy Ghost will "abide with you forever" (John 14:16). The Lord Jesus said also that the Holy Spirit, the third person of the Trinity, is the Agent who convicts and "reprove[s] the world of sin, and of righteousness, and of judgment" (John 16:8). Since the Holy Ghost must, therefore, be so ministering on the earth during the tribulation to the tremendous, numberless multitudes who will be convicted by Him of their sins, drawn by Him to Christ (John 6:44), saved by "the blood of the Lamb," and caught up to heaven "out of [that] great tribulation" (Revelation 7:14), it is not He, the Holy Spirit of God, who will "be taken out of the way" (2 Thessalonians 2:7), not even at the rapture of the church; but it is the church ("which is his body" [Ephesians 1:23; see also Colossians 1:18, 24; 1 Corinthians 12:27]) which is "he who now letteth [and] *will let*, until he [the Church, "the body of Christ" (1 Corinthians 12:13, 14, 27)] be taken out of the way [at the Rapture]" (2 Thessalonians 2:7). Without the presence and work of the Holy Ghost on earth, no one could be saved during the tribulation (John 16:7, 8; 6:44).

The promised Comforter teaches Christ's followers and causes them to remember His sayings: "But the Comforter, *which is* the Holy Ghost, whom the Father will send in my name, he shall teach you all things, and bring all things to your remembrance, whatsoever I have said unto you" (14:26).

The prophesied Comforter (the Holy Ghost, the Holy Spirit) is the real witness for Christ, working through the Christian: "But when the Comforter is come, whom I will send unto you from the Father, even the Spirit of truth, which proceedeth from the Father, he shall testify of me: And ye also shall bear witness [the power to witness was promised as a result of the Spirit baptism (Acts 1:8)], because ye have been with me from the beginning" (John 15:26, 27).

Jesus prophesied that He would have to depart—die on the cross, be resurrected and ascend to the Father—before the promised Holy Spirit would come, and that the Comforter would be the One who would convict the unrighteous of their sinful condition: "Nevertheless I tell you the truth; It is expedient for you that I go away: for if I go not away, the Comforter will not come unto you; but if I depart, I will send him unto you. And when he is come, he will reprove the world of sin, and of righteousness, and of judgment" (John 16:7, 8).

NOTE: Since it is the work of the Holy Spirit to convict the unsaved of their sinfulness, it is proper, when praying for one's unconverted friends and relatives, to ask Him to give them a conviction of sin, a desire to live righteously (in Christ), and a fear of judgment.

The Lord prophesied also that the "Spirit of truth" would guide His followers "into all truth," would show them "things to come," and would "glorify [Him]": "I have yet many things to say unto you, but ye cannot bear them now. Howbeit when he, the Spirit of truth, is come, he will guide you into all truth: for he shall not speak of himself; but whatsoever he shall hear, that shall he speak: and he will shew you things to come. He shall glorify me: for he shall receive of mine, and shall shew it unto you. All things that the Father hath are mine: therefore said I, that he shall take of mine, and shall shew it unto you" (John 16:12-15).

The Lord Jesus made the last prophecy concerning the first great outpouring of the Holy Ghost just before His ascension, and He gave His disciples that promise of great spiritual power to witness to and win souls for Him: "And being assembled together with them, commanded them that they should not depart from Jerusalem, but wait for the promise of the Father, which, saith he, ye have heard of me. For John truly baptized with water; but ye shall be baptized with the Holy Ghost not many days hence. . . . But ye shall receive power, after that the Holy Ghost is come upon you: and ye shall be witnesses unto me both in Jerusalem, and in all Judaea, and in Samaria, and unto the uttermost part of the earth" (Acts 1:4, 5, 8).

The First Mass Outpouring of the Holy Ghost With Visible, Audible Evidence

The first general outpouring of the Holy Ghost on disciples and apostles occurring in the New Testament was at Jerusalem on the Jewish feast Day of Pentecost, from the Greek word for "fifty," thus the fiftieth day from the offering of the firstfruits (Leviticus 23:15-16): "And when the day of Pentecost was fully come, they [the 120 of Acts 1:15] were all with one accord in one place. And suddenly there came a sound from heaven as of a rushing mighty wind, and it filled all the house where they were sitting [waiting, tarrying patiently, as Jesus had commanded them to do in Acts 1:4: "And, behold, I send the promise of my Father upon you: but tarry ye in the city of Jerusalem, until ye be endued with power from on high" (see also Luke 24:44)]. And there appeared unto them cloven tongues like as of fire, and it sat upon each of them. And they were all filled with the Holy Ghost [as foretold by the prophet Joel, in Joel 2:28, 29; by John the Baptist, in Matthew 3:11; Mark 1:7, 8, and Luke 3:16; and by the Lord Jesus Christ, in John 7:37-39, 15:26, 16:13; and in Acts 1:4, 5], and began to speak with other tongues [as foretold by Isaiah, over seven hundred years earlier, in Isaiah 28:11, 12; by Christ Jesus, in Mark 16:17; and referred to by Paul as a sign to unbelievers (a sign which would be rejected), in 1 Corinthains 14:21, 22] as the Spirit gave them utterance" (Acts 2:1-4).

Who were these already Spirit-begotten Christians who were baptized in the Holy Ghost on the Day of Pentecost with the Bible evidence of speaking "with other tongues as the Spirit gave them utterance" (v. 4)?

All of the 11 surviving Pentecostal apostles were present: "And when they were come in, they went up into an upper room, where abode Peter, and James, and John, and Andrew, Philip, and Thomas, Bartholamew and Matthew, James the son of Alphaeus, and Simon Zelotes, and Judas the brother of James" (Acts 1:13).

Mary, the mother of Jesus, the one hailed by the Catholics, who also became a Pentecostal, was there with other women: "These [the eleven apostles] all continued with one accord in prayer and supplicatoin with the women [probably "Mary Magdalene, and Mary the mother of James and Joses, and the mother of Zebedee's children" (Matthew 27:56)], and Mary the mother of Jesus, and

181

with his brethren. And in those days Peter stood up in the midst of the disciples . . . (number of names together were about an hundred and twenty)" (Acts 1:14, 15).

The outpouring of the Holy Ghost on this Day of Pentecost was visible and audible: "This Jesus hath God raised up, whereof we are all witnesses. Therefore being by the right hand of God exalted, and having received of the Father the promise of the Holy Ghost, he hath shed forth this, which ye now see and hear" (Acts 2:32, 33).

What did they "see and hear"? They *saw* the Spirit-baptized Christians drunk on the Spirit: "And they were all amazed, and were in doubt, saying one to another, What meaneth this? Others mocking said, These men are full of new wine. But Peter, standing up with the eleven, lifted up his voice, and said unto them, Ye men of Judaea, and all *ye* that dwell at Jerusalem. . . . these are not drunken, as ye suppose, seeing it is *but* the third hour of the day. But this is that which was spoken by the prophet Joel; And it shall come to pass in the last days, saith God, I will pour out of my Spirit upon all flesh" (Acts 2:12-17).

And they *heard* those Spirit-baptized, Spirit-filled disciples speak in other tongues: "And they were all filled with the Holy Ghost, and began to speak with other tongues, as the Spirit gave them utterance" (v. 4).

NOTE: It is important to realize that speaking in tongues—whether it relates to the baptism in the Holy Ghost (Acts 2:4; 10:46; 19:6), to the last two of the nine gifts of the Holy Spirit (1 Corinthians 12:7-11), or to one's individual religious devotions (14:14, 15, 28)—involves both the Holy Spirit, giving the utterance and the Christian doing the speaking, and is not an action undertaken freely, at will and alone by the Christian; there is always a dual participation: the Christian is anointed and given utterance by the Holy Ghost; but it is the Christian who speaks.

The duality of persons is further demonstrated in the fact that "the manifestation of the Spirit [the Holy Ghost, one entity] is given to every man [the Christian, the second entity] to profit withal" (12:7).

An additional example of the working together of both the Holy Spirit and man occurs in a listing of the gifts of the Spirit (vv. 8-11), including "divers kinds of tongues" (v. 10), the last verse of which states: "But all these worketh that one and the selfsame Spirit, dividing to every man severally as he will" (v. 11).

And, in yet another example, the Holy Spirit works hand in hand with and gives "utterance" to the Spirit-filled believer even in prayer ("For if I pray in an unknown tongue, my spirit prayeth. . . . I will pray with the spirit, and . . . with the understanding" [1 Corinthians 14:14, 15]), directing, inspiring and praying through the Christian, making "intercession for the saints according to the will of God" (Romans 8:27).

NOTE: Even though the apostle Paul said that tongues "are for a sign . . . to them that believe not" (1 Corinthains 14:22), there are still those who contend that the speaking in tongues in the Acts of the Apostles was necessary only, and was emphasized only, for the foreigners present to understand the gospel. This would not have been necessary at Ephesus (Acts 19:6), where the local language was the same for all of those who were baptized in the Holy Ghost. But speaking in tongues there was, as at Jerusalem, the initial evidence of the Spirit baptism. Neither was there a communication problem at the house of Cornelius (Acts 10:44-48), where those who received the baptism in the Holy Ghost and spoke in tongues apparently understood Peter without difficulty for they received the Holy Ghost while "Peter yet spake." Tongues again were the initial evidence of the Spirit baptism.

Besides their being the initial evidence of the baptism in the Holy Ghost, tongues also count as one of the nine gifts of the Holy Spirit (1 Corinthians 12:1-11). And more often than not, the born-again, Spirit-filled Christian who has been given the gift of "divers kinds of tongues" is not understood by the great majority of people, even by Spirit-filled Christians, who hear him or her exercise this gift of the Spirit: "For he that speaketh in an unknown tongue speaketh not unto men, but unto God: for no man understandeth him; howbeit in the spirit he speaketh mysteries" (14:2). That is the reason that a person who has been given the gift of the "interpretation of tongues" needs to be present: "If any man speak in an unknown tongue, let it be by two, or at the most by three, and that by course; and let one interpret" (v. 27).

It is true that, at the outpouring of the Holy Ghost on the Day of Pentecost, "there were dwelling at Jerusalem Jews, devout men, out of every nation under heaven" (Acts 2:5). However, according to Dr. John Nichols, one should note that the emphasis in this manifestation of the miracle of tongues was not necessarily limited to the speaking here but was probably on the hearing as well: "Behold, are not all these which speak Galilaeans? And how hear we every man in our own tongue, wherein we were born?" (vv. 7, 8).

Note that "every man," regardless of where he came from, heard the Galileans—emphasis is on the hearing— in his own language. Each Parthian stood by a Mede, who stood by an Elamite, who stood by a Mesopotamian, who stood by a Judaean, who stood by an Asian, who stood by a Cappadocian, who stood by a Pamphylian, who stood by a Phrygian, who stood by a Libyan, who stood by a Cyrenian, who stood by an Egyptian (see vv. 9-11); yet each one of them heard all of those who spoke in tongues in his "own tongue." (v. 87). "Every man [regardless of his birthplace] heard them [not just some of them?] speak [those who received the baptism in the Holy Ghost— "And they all were filled . . . and began to speak" (v. 4)] in his own language (v. 6). What did they hear? "[W]e do hear [emphasis on "hear"] them speak in our tongues the wonderful works of God" (v. 11).

Since these "devout men out of every nation" were "Jews," who "were dwelling ["inhabiting," "residing," "housing permanently," according to *Strong's Concordance*] at Jerusalem," it is most likely that they both spoke and understood the language of Peter, also a Jew, as well as the language of their country of origin (see, in *Dake's Annotated Reference Bible*, note *s* to Acts 2:5 and note *f* to Acts 2:14). Therefore the foreign tongues would probably not have been necessary *only* and solely for their understanding of the gospel but as a miracle ("[H]ow hear we [emphasis on "hear"] every man in our own tongue, wherein we were born?" [v. 8]) to convince them of the reality of the deity and messiahship of Christ, who was "[shedding] forth" the Holy Spirit here and whom Peter immediately thereafter preached (vv. 14-36), stating: "Therefore being by the right hand of God exalted, and having received of the Father the promise of the Holy Ghost, he hath shed forth this, which ye now see and hear" (v. 33). How would they have understood Peter's sermon, which was not in miraculous tongues, unless they understood the language spoken by the Jews? A lot of them certainly must have understood—3,000 were saved on that very day.

The Second Recorded Infilling of Newborn Believers

The second major outpouring of the Holy Ghost occurred at Samaria, after Philip's revival, about one year after the mass outpouring at Jerusalem: "Then laid they *their* hands on them, and they received the Holy Ghost" (8:17).

NOTE: This is the only specifically mentioned major infilling in Acts where it says that believers initially received the Holy Ghost without its indicating that they spoke in tongues. However, the writer of Acts had already mentioned that there was "great joy in the city;" and he lists experiences that involved essentially all nine of the gifts of the Spirit (see 1 Corinthians 12:1-11), except "tongues" and "interpretation of tongues."

There were manifested in Samaria the "gifts of healings" ("and many taken with palsies, and that were lame, were healed" [Acts 8:7]) and the "working of miracles" ("hearing and seeing the miracles [miracles can be seen and heard!] which he did" [v. 6]), both of which manifestations accompanied Philip's supernatural use of the divine "word of knowledge": "And the people with one accord gave heed unto those things which Philip spake [he was unusually perceptive in his knowledge of God and His Word—the Samaritan revival proves it], hearing and seeing the miracles" (8:6).

The "gift of faith" was evident in verses 6, 7 and 13 ("beholding the miracles [miracle working faith] and signs which were done" [v. 13]); the discerning of spirits in verse 7 ("For unclean spirits, crying with loud voice, came out of many that were possessed with them"); the "gift of prophecy" in verses 5, 6 and 12 ("But when they believed Philip preaching the things concerning the king- dom of God ["things" now and in the future], and the name of Jesus Christ, they were baptized, both men and women" [v.12]); and the "word of wisdom," which was demonstrated in the God-given wisdom of Philip through- out the very successful Samaritan revival of supernatural power and gifts.

Yet, for none of these gifts did Simon the Sorcerer ever offer money; but, "when Simon saw [he observed and/or heard something] that through laying on of the apostles' hands the Holy Ghost was given, he offered them money, Saying, Give me also this power, that on whomsoever I lay hands, he may receive the Holy Ghost" (vv. 18, 19). There was apparently some manifestation of God's Spirit here that Simon had not previously seen. And he had already had occasion to see essentially all of the nine gifts of the Holy Ghost in evidence during the Samaritan revival except the gifts of "tongues [and] interpretation of tongues" (1 Corinthians 12:10), which would indicate, with great probability, that Philip's Samaritan converts spoke in tongues. *The Pulpit Commentary* (XVIII, 280) hints at this same conclusion: "These points assume that the indications of the Spirit's coming on the disciples were such as we find at Pentecost. There was some gift of tongues, or preaching, or praying—some outward sign which all could realize." The statement in *Barnes' Notes* on this spiritual incident is even more firmly in agreement with the aforementioned conclusion: "*Simon saw*, etc. That is, he witnessed the extraordinary effects, the power of speaking in a miraculous manner, etc." (X, 142). "It was something that was discernible *by external effects*; for Simon *saw...* the power of speaking with new tongues" (X, 141).

To this evidence add the fact that the initial part of the Spirit baptism experience at Ephesus—"And when Paul had laid his hands upon them, the Holy Ghost came on them; and they spake with tongues, and prophesied" (Acts 19:6)—was almost exactly the same as that at Samaria: "Then laid they their hands on them, and they received the Holy Ghost" (8:17). Did the Samaritan converts speak in tongues? The Lord Jesus prophesied that a mark of believers would be speaking "with new tongues": "And these signs shall follow them that believe . . . they shall speak with new tongues" (Mark 16:17).

Another similarity is noted in the Samaritan experience with that on the Day of Pentecost, prayer preceding the infilling: "These all continued with one accord in prayer and supplication, with the women, and Mary the mother of Jesus, and with his brethren. . . . And when the day of Pentecost was fully come, they were all with one accord in one place. . . . And they were all filled with the Holy Ghost, and began to speak with other tongues, as the Spirit gave them utterance" (Acts 1:14; 2:1, 4). "Who [Peter and John], when they were come down, prayed for them, that they might receive the Holy Ghost. . . . Then laid they their hands on them, and they received the Holy Ghost" (8:15, 17).

Yet another parallel in terminology occurs in the experience at the house of Cornelius—"While Peter yet spake these words, the Holy Ghost fell on all them. . . . [How did they know?] For they heard them speak with tongues, and magnify God" (10:44, 46)—with the Samaritan experience, in both of which instances the writer speaks of the Holy Spirit falling on believers: "(For as yet he was fallen upon none of them. . . .) Then laid they *their* hands on them, and they received the Holy Ghost" (8:16, 17).

What was the evidence of the Spirit baptism in the latter case? Isaiah prophesied that speaking with stammering lips and in other tongues would be an indication of a spiritual experience that Jehovah was promising as a great rest and a great refreshing to aid the spiritually weary who would accept it, especially and specifically in the church age: "For with stammering lips and another tongue will he speak to this people. To whom he said, This is the rest wherewith ye may cause the weary to rest; and this is the refreshing [But would the world of unbelievers accept this sign?]: yet they would not hear" (Isaiah 28:11, 12).

The apostle Paul, in his chapter on the spiritual gift of tongues, makes reference to Isaiah's prophecy: "In the law [the Old Testament] it is written, With men of other tongues and other lips will I speak unto this people; and yet for all that will they not hear me [note the rejection by unbelievers as prophesied by Isaiah], saith the Lord" (1 Corinthians 14:21). And, in the next verse, Paul underscores the fact that the gift of speaking in tongues was, and is, a specific sign to these same unbelievers who reject it: "Wherefore tongues are for a sign, not to them that believe, but to them that believe not" (v. 22).

Note also that such experts as Peter and John, who were present when the Samaritan Christians were baptized in the Holy Ghost, did not question the validity of their experience. Both of these apostles spoke in tongues on the Day of Pentecost: "And they were all filled with the Holy Ghost, and began to speak with other tongues, as the Spirit gave them utterance" (Acts 2:4). And Peter and John came down to Samaria specifically to see that Philip's new converts received the same experience: "Who [Peter and John] prayed for them, that they might receive the Holy Ghost. . . . Then laid they their hands on them, and they received the Holy Ghost" (Acts 8:15, 17).

And since the apostle Peter, who was much later reprimanded by the Jews at Jerusalem for preaching to the Gentiles at the house of Cornelius (11:1-18), would validate those Gentiles' experience by describing it as being the same as that of the disciples on the Day of Pentecost ("And as I began to speak, the Holy Ghost fell on them, as on us at the beginning [no mention here of tongues, but the phenomenon of glossolalia certainly occurred (see Acts 2:4)]" [Acts 11:15]), would he not have invalidated the Samaritan experience if it had not been sufficiently similar to that at Pentecost?

With this weighty evidence, it is difficult to arrive at any other conclusion than that the Samaritan believers spoke in tongues on being filled with the Holy Ghost.

The Outpouring of the Holy Ghost on the Gentile Believers at the House of Cornelius

Approximately 10 years after the Pentecostal outpouring in Jerusalem, the Holy Ghost fell on the first Gentile believers in the home of Cornelius, the Roman centurion: "While Peter yet spake these words, the Holy Ghost fell on all them which heard the word. And they of the circumcision [the six Jews who had accompanied Peter (Acts 11:12)] which believed were astonished, as many as came with Peter, because that on the Gentiles also was poured out the gift of the Holy Ghost. [How did these Jews know that these Gentiles had received "the gift of the Holy Ghost"?]. For they heard them speak with tongues, and magnify God. Then answered Peter, Can any man forbid water, that these should not be baptized, which have received the Holy Ghost as well as we? And he commanded them to be baptized in the name of the Lord" (Acts 10:44-48).

NOTE: It is important to recall here that baptismal regenerationists, both the non-Pentecostal Trinitarians and the Pentecostal non-Trinitarians, as previously indicated, place extremely heavy emphasis on the tenet that water baptism saves souls.

It should be noted that the sequence of Simon Peter's commands to the Jews on the Day of Pentecost was to "Repent, and be baptized . . . in the name of Jesus Christ" before receiving "the gift of the Holy Ghost" (2:38). Dr. Ray H. Hughes calls attention to the fact that this sequence was reversed, however, during the anointed preaching of the same apostle Peter at the house of Cornelius, the Roman centurion, who, with his Gentile household, was unsaved before Peter, with six Jews, brought him and his kinsmen and friends the gospel (11:12-14).

Dr. Hughes points out that Peter preached (10:34-43), and the Gentiles believed (Acts 11:17), repented (11:18), were saved by receiving "remission of [their] sins" (10:43), were baptized in the Holy Ghost (v. 44), spoke "with tongues" (v. 46), and, last of all, were commanded to be baptized in water (vv. 47, 48), indicating that salvation is not absolutely dependent on water baptism—which is simply a figure of the death, burial and resurrection of the Lord Jesus Christ and "the answer of [an already] good conscience toward God"—since these Gentiles were already saved, justified, sanctified and filled with the Holy Spirit before they were baptized in water (see 1 Corinthians 1:14-21).

NOTE: The Pentecostal non-Trinitarians also teach that the sacrament of water baptism must, unalterably, be done in the name of "Jesus only," instead of the Trinity, in order for it to be valid. This teaching—based on a 1914 revelation and, possibly, partially on Acts 2:38 ("be baptized . . . in the name of Jesus Christ")—lacks Biblical support.

The Lord Jesus Christ, who was Emmanuel, "God with us," and who, therefore, could not lie, was undoubtedly the best and final authority on the formula for water baptism; and He commanded His disciples to baptize "in the name of the Father, and of the Son, and of the Holy Ghost" (Matthew 28:19).

Peter said, on the Day of Pentecost, to baptize "in the name of Jesus Christ" (Acts 2:38). Philip's Samaritan converts "were baptized in the name of the Lord Jesus,"

(8:16), as were the Ephesian disciples of John (19:5). And the Gentile converts at the house of Cornelius received water baptism, not just in the name of "Jesus only" but, "in the name of the Lord" (10:48), which can refer to the Father (2 Corinthians 6:18), or to the Son (1 Corinthians 8:6), or to the Holy Ghost (Acts 28:25, 26; see also Isaiah 6:8, 9).

There are four listed formulae, then, for water baptism: (1) "in the name of the Father, and of the Son, and of the Holy Ghost" (Matthew 28:19, by Jesus, who was, as already indicated, the best or only real authority, since He was "God with us" [Matthew 1:23]); (2) "in the name of Jesus Christ" (Acts 2:38, by Peter, on the Day of Pentecost, who, according to *Dake's Annotated Reference Bible* [see p. 124 of the New Testament, right column, note *a*; p. 135, right column, note *m*; and p. 146, left column, note *i*] meant "by the authority of Jesus Christ," which baptism to a Jewish convert also meant the loss of all of his Jewish rights and privileges and his Jewish friends—a lot to give up to follow a lowly Nazarene whom most Jews rejected as the Messiah); (3) "in the name of the Lord Jesus" (8:12, 13, 16, by Philip and/or Peter and John at Samaria and 19:5, by Paul at Ephesus, all of whom, again, meant "by the authority of the Lord Jesus"); and (4) "in the name of the Lord" (10:48, by Peter at the house of Cornelius).

The non-Trinitarian Pentecostals have debated Trinitarians for years about and have written volumes on the efficacy of water baptism just "in the NAME of JESUS" (see Oliver F. Fauss, *Baptism in God's Plan* [Hazelwood, Missouri: Pentecostal Publishing House, 1955], p. 37; and John Paterson, *The Real Truth About Baptism in*

Jesus' Name [same publisher, 1953], pp. 20, 21), empha-
sizing that "[w]e must be baptized in Jesus' name [to be
saved]— for 'neither is there salvation in any other: for
there is none other name under heaven given among men
whereby we MUST be saved' (Acts 4:12)" (in Paterson,
p. 21). See Carl Brumback, a Trinitarian, (*God in Three
Persons* [Cleveland, Tennessee: Pathway Press, 1959], p.
11ff.) for confirmation of this Oneness tenet: "Unless the
words, 'I baptize you in the name of Jesus Christ,' were
spoken by the minister, the salvation of the baptized one
was endangered."

But note that the apostle Peter—whose Pentecostal
formula in Acts 2:38 ("be baptized . . . in the name of
Jesus Christ") became, essentially, that formula of revelation in 1914 (Brumback, pp. 11, 12) of the non-Trinitarian
Pentecostals and who (Peter) was involved in three out of
four of the major infillings and baptisms in Acts—apparently
neither had nor followed any set, rigid or regular formula for water baptism.

Peter's publicly declared baptismal formula at the
Pentecostal outpouring (Acts 2:1-40) was "in the name of
Jesus Christ" (v. 38); however, those 3,000 souls saved at
Pentecost "were baptized" (vv. 41) without any indica-
tion of formulaic importance.

And again, Peter, who came down to Samaria with
John with the purpose of praying for Philip's revival converts "to receive the Holy Ghost" (8:14, 15), made no
recorded comment on the slight change or difference in
formula used there: "in the name of the Lord Jesus" (v. 16).

And, lastly, Peter's command to the Gentile converts at
the house of Cornelius (10:44-48) was "to be baptized in the
name of the Lord" (v. 48)—which, as previously indicated,

can refer to the Father (2 Corinthians 6:18), or to the Son (1 Corinthians 8:6), or to the Holy Ghost (Isaiah 6:8, 9 with Acts 28:25, 26)—the third different formula used in just three important baptizings in Acts where Peter was involved with the converts, indicating again that Peter had no consistent formulaic phrase that he used or recommended for water baptism.

Upon weighing the choices, a Christian could only choose the formula commanded by the Lord Jesus Christ, the promised Messiah, who was "God with us" (Matthew 1:23); who was called by the prophet "the mighty God" (Isaiah 9:6); who as "the Word was God" (John 1:1); who, to "doubting" Thomas, was "my Lord and my God" (20:28); who, according to Paul, was "in very nature God" (Philippians 2:6, *NIV*); who was the One "in [whom] dwelleth all the fulness of the Godhead bodily" (Colossians 2:9); and who was the One whom even the Father called God: "Thy throne, O God, is for ever and ever" (Hebrews 1:8). What better authority for the deity of Christ could one have than God the Father himself? What better authority for a baptismal formula could one follow than that of God the Son himself (in Matthew 28:19), the "Alpha and Omega, the beginning and the ending . . . which is, and which was, and which is to come, the Almighty" (Revelation 1:8), the One to whom was given "All power [or "authority"] . . . in heaven and in earth" (Matthew 28:18)?

The Spirit Baptism of the Longtime Disciples at Ephesus

Approximately 25 years after the outpouring on the Day of Pentecost at Jerusalem, "the Holy Ghost came on" a dozen or so disciples of John the Baptist at Ephesus: "He [Paul] said unto them, Have ye received the Holy Ghost since ye believed? And they said unto him, We have not so much as heard whether there be any Holy Ghost. . . . And when Paul had laid his hands on them, the Holy Ghost came on them; and they spake with tongues, and prophesied. And all the men were about twelve" (Acts 19:2, 6, 7).

NOTE: The Spirit baptism of these believers years and years after the initial Pentecostal experience, which occurred shortly after the ascension of Christ ("It is expedient for you that I go away: for if I go not away, the Comforter will not come unto you; but if I depart, I will send him [another member of the Trinity] unto you" [John 16:7]), emphasizes the fact that (1) the baptism in the Holy Spirit did not cease on or soon after the Pentecostal outpouring and that (2) the baptism in the Holy Ghost was not limited to the 12 apostles. The outpouring at the house of Cornelius, the centurion, where even Gentiles received the Holy Ghost baptism (Acts 10:9-48), further substantiates the latter of these two points.

The prophecy of Joel—which is cited by Peter—concerning the time of the outpouring of the Holy Spirit is another scripture which supports the teaching that this experience of the enduement of power for witnessing did not cease with the occurrence at Ephesus or with any other recorded example of the Holy Spirit baptism: "But this is that which was spoken by the prophet Joel; And it shall come to pass in the last days ["afterward" in Joel 2:28: anytime after Israel's restoration], saith God, I will pour out of my Spirit upon all flesh [no person excepted]: and your sons [not just adult apostles or disciples] and your daughters [not just men and boys] shall prophesy, and your young men shall see visions, and your old men [even the senior adults who still desire to be of profitable service to Christ's cause] shall dream dreams: And on my servants and on my hand maidens [another confirmation of lady preachers] I will pour out in those days of my Spirit; and they shall prophesy [*prophesying* is defined by Paul in 1 Corinthians 14:3 as "edification, and exhortation, and comfort" and not just as foretelling future events]" (Acts 2:16-18).

"And. . . . I will pour out in those days of my Spirit." Which days? The last days, of which the Day of Pentecost was only the beginning (Acts 2: 16, 17), continued with the outpourings down through the end-time centuries, as recorded in histories and encyclopedias, with the widespread Holy Spirit baptisms during the last two decades of the 19th century (especially in western North Carolina and eastern Tennessee), and then with the great Azusa Street spiritual outpouring and revival in Los Angeles and with other such outpourings around the world in the early years of the 20th century. This still continues with the present-day outpourings in almost every country in the world, including the vast and heavily populated, mostly atheistic, country of Communist China. All these events continue in these present days, days which are even more nearly, much more nearly the "afterward" times or "last days" than were those days when Peter preached the power-packed soulwinning message at Pentecost in Jerusalem more nearly the last days; or than when Philip, the layman (6:1-5) preached it at Samaria; than when Peter preached it (again) at the house of Cornelius, the Gentile; than when Paul preached it at Ephesus.

197

And God's born-again, Spirit-begotten converts who desire more power to witness will continue to be baptized in the Holy Ghost even on into those future "last days," even those saved during the tribulation period—as also mentioned by Joel in this same prophecy (Joel 2:28-32; note vv. 30-32) and quoted by Peter (Acts 2:16-21; note vv. 19-21)—when, endued with God's spiritual power to witness, they will testify to and win "a great multitude, which no man [can] number, of all nations, and kindreds, and people, and tongues, [who will stand] before the throne, and before the Lamb, clothed with white robes, and palms in their hands. . . . These are they which came out of great tribulation" (Revelation 7:9, 14).

Zechariah's prophecy concerning the Battle of Armageddon at the end of the Tribulation and the return of the Messiah, Christ Jesus with pierced hands, who will fight against and defeat the Antichrist (14:1-3) supports the prediction of Joel that the outpouring of the Holy Ghost will extend into, indeed up to the end of, the Great Tribulation: "And I will pour upon the house of David, and upon the inhabitants of Jerusalem, the spirit of grace and supplications: and they shall look upon me whom they have pierced, and they shall mourn for him, as one mourneth for his only son, and shall be in bitterness for him, as one that is in bitterness for his firstborn" (Zechariah 12:10). The outpourings will not even cease then. In the millennium, when "[K]ing [Jesus] shall reign in righteousness" (Isaiah 32:1), "the spirit [will] be poured upon us from on high [sounds like Luke 24:49], and the wilderness [will] be a fruitful field" (Isaiah 32:15).

The "last days" outpourings of God's Holy Spirit, as prophesied in Joel 2:28-32 and confirmed by Peter in

Acts 2:16-21, with the Biblical evidence of speaking in other tongues "as the spirit gave them utterance," as prophesied in Isaiah 28:11, 12, and Mark 16:17, still have 1,007 years—at least—to go: through both the tribulation and the millennium.

NOTE: Some claim and teach, that, for various reasons, tongues ceased during the latter part of the first century and, consequently, as already indicated, so did the Pentecostal experience of the baptism in the Holy Spirit. This doctrine is based on 1 Corinthians 13:8-10 which says: "Charity never faileth: but whether there be prophecies, they shall fail; whether there be tongues, they shall cease; whether there be knowledge, it shall vanish away. For we know in part, and we prophesy in part. But when that which is perfect is come, then that which is in part shall be done away."

Their teaching is, usually, that with the writing of the New Testament books and/or the establishment of the early churches "that which is perfect" had come and that there was no need for "that which is in part," which included tongues. However, knowledge has not yet vanished away: those who claim that tongues have ceased use knowledge in reaching that conclusion; and preaching or prophesying— defined by Paul in the very next chapter (1 Corinthians 14:3) as "edification, and exhortation, and comfort" and not necessarily as foretelling the future only—is still being practiced by some of those very same ministers who reject the Pentecostal experience with its Biblical evidence of speaking in tongues (Acts 2:4; 10:44-46; 19:6).

Whatever "that which is perfect" is—and there is some disagreement and uncertainty about it—it seems, according to 1 Corinthians 13:12, that it refers to the future heavenly state of Christians "when this corruptible shall have put on incorruption, and this mortal shall have put on immortality" (1 Corinthians 15:54, the resurrection chapter); a time when we shall no longer "see through a glass, darkly" and no longer "know in part;" a time when earthly or partial "knowledge . . . shall vanish away;" when prophesying/preaching—no longer needed "shall fail;" and when tongues—no longer essential as a spiritually miraculous "sign . . . to them that believe not" (who, not believing in Christ and not trusting in Him alone for salvation, jeopardize their eternal future) (1 Corinthians 14:22)— "shall cease" or be stilled, as Paul so prophesied (13:8).

But until that time "when that which is perfect is come," Paul counsels the "brethren": "[1] covet to prophesy ["that the church may receive edifying"? (1 Corinthains 14:3, 4, 5)], and [2] forbid not to speak with tongues [as "a sign . . . to them that believe not"? (vv. 21, 22) as well as a means, when interpreted, of edifying the church? (vv. 5, 26-28)]. [3] Let all things be done decently and in order [so that the "unlearned" or "unbelievers" "will . . . not say that ye are mad"? (23, 26-28, 32, 33)]" (vv. 39, 40).

NOTE: The Spirit baptism of the Ephesian believers ("Have ye received the Holy Ghost since ye believed?" [Acts 19:2]) shows that the birth of the Spirit (John 3:3, 5), which gives the believer power for sonship (John 1:12, 13; see also Romans 8:9, 14-16), does not always or necessarily occur simultaneously with the baptism in the Holy Spirit, which gives the believer power for witnessing (Acts 1:8). It is important to note that the disciples who received the Spirit baptism on the Day of Pentecost were already born again, for they already had their names written in heaven (Luke 10:20; see also Exodus 32:33; Revelation 20:15, 10); that the Samaritan converts, a year later, were already believers and were thus born again (Acts 8:12) before they received the Holy Ghost (Acts 8:15-17); that the apostle Paul had already called upon "the name of the Lord" (Acts 9:5, 6, 11; see also Acts 2:21 and Romans 10:13) and was considered a born-again brother before Ananias informed him that he was to "be filled with the Holy Ghost" (Acts 9:17); and as already indicated, that the Ephesian disciples had been saved, believing disciples (Acts 19:1, 2), as a result of John's preaching (Mark 1:2-5), for as many as 25 years before "the Holy Ghost came on them; and they spake with tongues, and prophesied" (Acts 19:6).

REVIEW OF IMPORTANT SCRIPTURES ON THE BAPTISM IN THE HOLY GHOST

1. *The baptism in the Holy Ghost and its rejection are foretold.* Probably the earliest prophecy of the spiritual blessings and the Biblical evidence of the last-days out-pouring of and baptism in the Holy Spirit—and its rejection—is made by Isaiah: "For with stammering lips and another tongue will he speak to this people. To whom he said, This is the rest wherewith ye may cause the weary to rest; and this is the refreshing: yet they would not hear" (Isaiah 28:11, 12).

Paul refers to this refreshing spiritual experience—along with its rejection—as a sign to unbelievers in his instructional chapter on tongues and interpretations: "In the law it is written, with men of other tongues and other lips will I speak unto this people; and yet for all that will they not hear me, saith the Lord. Wherefore tongues are for a sign, not to them that believe, but to them that believe not" (1 Corinthians 14:21, 22).

2. *The baptism in the Holy Ghost empowers the Christian to witness for Christ.* This baptism of witnessing power often comes after prayer: "And when they had prayed, the place was shaken where they were assembled together; and they were all filled with the Holy Ghost, and they spake the word of God with boldness. . . . And with great power gave the apostles witness of the resurrection of the Lord Jesus" (Acts 4:31, 33; note also 1:14; 2:1-4; 8:15, 17).

3. *Every Christian is to be a witness for Christ.* To witness for (to confess) Christ is the duty of every newly converted Christian and a resultant phase of his conversion: "That shalt confess with thy mouth the Lord Jesus, and shalt believe in thine heart that God hath raised him from the dead, thou shalt be saved" (Romans 10:9).

To witness for (to bear testimony of) Christ is a means of overcoming the devil: "And they overcame him [the devil] by the blood of the Lamb, and by the word of their testimony" (Revelation 12:11).

To witness for Christ was the commandment of the Lord: "[A]nd ye shall be witnesses unto me both in Jerusalem, and in all Judaea, and in Samaria, and unto the uttermost part of the earth" (Acts 1:8).

4. *The Christian needs power to be an effective witness for Christ.* Christians receive power to become sons of God as a result of being born of the Holy Spirit (Holy Ghost): "But as many as received him, to them gave he power to

become the sons of God, *even* to them that believe on his name: Which were born . . . of God" (John 1:12, 13; see also John 3:3-5).

But Christians receive power to witness for Christ as a result of the baptism (outpouring, gift, filling) of the Holy Ghost (Holy Spirit): "But ye shall receive power, after that the Holy Ghost is come upon you: and ye shall be witnesses unto me both in Jerusalem, and in all Judaea, and in Samaria, and unto the uttermost part of the earth" (Acts 1:8).

The early followers of Christ and the apostles received this power to witness: "And with great power gave the apostles witness of the resurrection of the Lord Jesus" (Acts 4:33).

Paul, who was converted after the resurrection of Christ, received this power and a command to witness: "And Ananias went his way, and entered into the house; and putting his hands on him [Ananias was not one of the twelve disciples] said, Brother Saul, the Lord, even Jesus, that appeared unto thee in the way as thou camest, hath sent me, that thou mightest receive thy sight, and be filled with the Holy Ghost" (Acts 9:17). "For thou shalt be his witness unto all men of what thou hast seen and heard" (22:15).

Did Paul ever speak in tongues? "I thank my God, I speak with tongues more than ye all" (1 Corinthians 14:18).

The Holy Ghost (Holy Spirit, Comforter) then is the real witness for Christ, working through the Christian: "But when the Comforter is come, whom I will send unto you from the Father, even the Spirit of truth, which proceedeth from the Father, he shall testify of me" (John 15:26).

203

The Holy Ghost aids the Christian to be an effective witness for Christ by bringing to his mind the words of Christ, the scriptures to be used: "But the Comforter, *which* is the Holy Ghost, whom the Father will send in my name, he shall teach you all things, and bring all things to your remembrance, whatsoever I have said unto you" (John 14:26).

5. *The baptism in the Holy Ghost, which brings power to witness, was foretold.* The outpouring of the Holy Ghost was foretold by an old testament prophet: "And it shall come to pass afterward, that I will pour out my spirit upon all flesh; and your sons and your daughters shall prophesy, your old men shall dream dreams, your young men shall see visions: And also upon the servants and upon the handmaids in those days will I pour out my spirit" (Joel 2:28, 29). (Note the fulfillment in Acts 2:16-21.)

The baptism of the Holy Ghost was foretold by John the Baptist: "I indeed have baptized you with water: but he shall baptize you with the Holy Ghost" (Mark 1:8; see also Matthew 3:11; Luke 3:16; John 1:33).

6. *The gift of the Holy Ghost was foretold by Jesus.* "And I [one of the divine Trinity, called God in Hebrews 1:8] will pray the Father [another of the divine Trinity, called God in John 6:27], and he shall give you another Comforter [the third member of the divine Trinity, called God in Acts 5:3, 4], that he may abide with you for ever; Even the Spirit of truth; whom the world cannot receive, because it seeth him not, neither knoweth him: but ye know him; for he dwelleth with you, and shall be in you" (John 14:16, 17). "For John truly baptized with water; but ye shall be baptized with the Holy Ghost not many days hence" (Acts 1:5).

7. *The prophecy of the outpouring began to be fulfilled with visible, audible evidence.* The Holy Ghost was first poured out on disciples and apostles on the Jewish Feast Day of Pentecost: "And when the Day of Pentecost was fully come, they were all with one accord in one place. And suddenly there came a sound from heaven as of a rushing mighty wind, and it filled all the house where they were sitting. And there appeared unto them cloven tongues like as of fire, and it sat upon each of them. And they were all filled with the Holy Ghost, and began to speak with other tongues, as the Spirit gave them utterance" (Acts 2:1-4). "This Jesus hath God raised up, whereof we all are witnesses. Therefore being by the right hand of God exalted, and having received of the Father the promise of the Holy Ghost, he hath shed forth this, which ye now see [visible] and hear [audible]" (vv. 32, 33).

The second recorded filling of newborn believers occurred at Samaria about one year later: "Then laid they their hands on them, and they received the Holy Ghost" (Acts 8:17).

Approximately 10 years after the Pentecostal outpouring, the Holy Ghost fell on the Gentile believers at the house of Cornelius: "While Peter yet spake these words, the Holy Ghost fell on all them which heard the word. And they of the circumcision which believed were astonished, as many as came with Peter, because that on the Gentiles also was poured out the gift of the Holy Ghost. [How did they know?] For they heard them speak with tongues, and magnify God" (Acts 10:44-46). "And as I began to speak, the Holy Ghost fell on them, as on us at the beginning [on the Day of Pentecost]. Then remembered

I the word of the Lord, how that he said, John indeed baptized with water; but ye shall be baptized with the Holy Ghost" (11:15, 16).

Some 25 years after the first outpouring, the Holy Ghost came on some longtime disciples at Ephesus: "And when Paul [not one of the twelve disciples] had laid his hands upon them, the Holy Ghost came on them; and they spake with tongues, and prophesied" (19:6).

8. *Speaking in tongues is an evident sign.* Speaking in (new, unknown or other) tongues is a sign to the unbelievers: "Wherefore tongues are for a sign, not to them that believe, but to them that believe not" (1 Corinthians 14:22).

Speaking in tongues was foretold by Jesus as a sign which was to follow believers: "And these signs shall follow them that believe; In my name shall they cast out devils; they shall speak with new tongues" (Mark 16:17).

Speaking in tongues was foretold by an Old Testament prophet, who prophesied also that it would not be accepted: "For with stammering lips and another tongue will he speak to this people. To whom he said, This is the rest wherewith ye may cause the weary to rest; and this is the refreshing: yet they would not hear" (Isaiah 28:11, 12).

Paul referred to Isaiah's prophecy that this sign would not be accepted: "In the law it is written, With men of other tongues and other lips will I speak unto this people; and yet for all that will they not hear me, saith the Lord" (1 Corinthians 14:21).

9. *Every believer should seek to be filled with the Holy Ghost.* The believer may receive the baptism in the Holy Ghost as soon as he is saved: "Who shall tell thee words,

whereby thou and all thy house shall be saved (Cornelius was unsaved before Peter preached]. And as I began to speak, the Holy Ghost fell on them, as on us at the beginning [just like the experience at Pentecost] (Acts 11:14, 15).

The believer may receive the baptism in the Holy Ghost a short time after salvation: "Who, when they were come down, prayed for them, that they might receive the Holy Ghost: (For as yet he was fallen upon none of them: only they were baptized in the name of the Lord Jesus.) Then laid they *their* hands on them, and they received the Holy Ghost" (8:15-17).

There may be a long interval between salvation and the baptism in the Holy Ghost: "He said unto them, Have ye received the Holy Ghost since ye believed? [Or did you receive the Holy Ghost when you believed?] And they said unto him, We have not so much as heard whether there be any Holy Ghost. And he said unto them, Unto what then were you baptized? And they said, Unto John's baptism. Then said Paul, John verily baptized with the baptism of repentance, saying unto the people, that they should believe on him which should come after him, that is, on Christ Jesus. When they heard this, they were baptized in the name of the Lord Jesus. And when Paul had laid his hands upon them, the Holy Ghost came on them; and they spake with tongues, and prophesied" (19:2-6).

The believer may be baptized in water before receiving the baptism in the Holy Ghost: "(For as yet he was fallen upon none of them: only they were baptized in the name of the Lord Jesus.) Then laid they their hands on them, and they received the Holy Ghost" (8:16, 17).

The believer may be baptized in water after having been saved, sanctified, justified, and after having received the baptism in the Holy Ghost, showing that water baptism is not that element which saves souls: "Can any man forbid water, that these should not be baptized, which have received the Holy Ghost as well as we? And he commanded them to be baptized in the name of the Lord" (10:47, 48).

The dedicated believer may be refilled with the Holy Ghost from time to time: "Then Peter, filled with the Holy Ghost, said unto them" (Acts 4:8). "And when they had prayed, the place was shaken where they were assembled together; and they were all filled with the Holy Ghost, and they spake the word of God with boldness" (v. 31). "And the disciples were filled with joy, and with the Holy Ghost" (13:52).

The believer does not have to be an apostle or a full-time minister to be filled with the Holy Ghost: "Then the twelve called the multitude of the disciples unto them, and said, It is not reason that we should leave the word of God, and serve tables. Wherefore, brethren, look ye out among you seven men of honest report, full of the Holy Ghost and wisdom, whom we may appoint over this business. But we will give ourselves continually to prayer, and to the ministry of the word" (6:2-4).

10. *The baptism in the Holy Ghost is available to all believers during this the church age.* The Spirit of God was restricted to select spiritual leaders during the Old Testament times: "And Moses said unto him, Enviest thou for my sake? would God that all the Lord's people were prophets, and that the Lord would put his spirit upon them!" (Numbers 11:29).

But the baptism in the Holy Ghost is promised to all during this dispensation: "And it shall come to pass in the last days, saith God, I will pour out of my Spirit upon all flesh: and your sons and your daughters shall prophesy" (Acts 2:17).

The baptism in the Holy Ghost was promised to every believer all down through the church age: "Then Peter said unto them, Repent, and be baptized every one of you in the name of Jesus Christ for the remission of sins, and ye shall receive the gift of the Holy Ghost. For the promise is unto you, and to your children, and to all that are afar off, even as many as the Lord our God shall call" (vv. 38, 39).

The baptism in the Holy Ghost is for those who are obedient: "And we are his witnesses of these things; and so is also the Holy Ghost, whom God hath given to them that obey him" (5:32).

The baptism in the Holy Ghost is for those who pray persistently, who importune: "If ye then, being evil, know how to give good gifts unto your children: how much more shall your heavenly Father give the Holy Spirit to them that ask him?" (Luke 11:13; see vv. 5-13.)

The baptism in the Holy Ghost is for those who tarry, who wait on God: "And, behold, I send the promise of my Father upon you: but tarry ye in the city of Jerusalem, until ye be endued with power from on high" (Luke 24:49). "And, being assembled together with them, commanded them that they should not depart from Jerusalem, but wait for the promise of the Father, which, saith he, ye have heard of me" (Acts 1:4).

11. *The real purpose, then, of the baptism in the Holy Ghost, is to empower the believer to tell the story of Jesus*

to the lost and unsaved. The Holy Ghost gives the believer power to become an effective witness for Christ: "But ye shall receive power, after that the Holy Ghost is come upon you: and ye shall be witnesses unto me . . . unto the uttermost part of the earth" (Acts 1:8).

The believer whose power and boldness to witness have waned or whose power and boldness need to be increased may be refilled with the Holy Ghost: "And when they [this "they" includes Peter and John and other very consecrated disciples who were filled and spoke in tongues on the Day of Pentecost] had prayed, the place was shaken where they were assembled together; and they were all filled with the Holy Ghost, and they spake the word of God with boldness" (Acts 4:31).

SPEAKING
IN TONGUES

In his prophecy on speaking in tongues, Isaiah indicated that this last-days spiritual experience would be a delightful one, a restful and refreshing experience: "For with stammering lips and another tongue will he speak to this people. To whom he said, This is the rest wherewith ye may cause the weary to rest; and this is the refreshing: yet they would not hear" (Isaiah 28:11, 12). The disciples who received the Spirit baptism on the Day of Pentecost were so happy and joyful that the amazed onlookers thought that they were "full of new wine" (Acts 2:13). The Gentiles at the house of Cornelius were so spiritually blessed that they began to "speak with tongues, and [praise and] magnify God" (10:46). When "the Holy Ghost came on" the Ephesian disciples of John "they spake with tongues" and exploded into spiritually prophetic and anointed preaching (19:6). And Paul and Barnabas—on being expelled from Antioch, right in the midst of persecution—"were filled with joy [God is always there to bless His people with the Holy Ghost, even in the worst of situations], and with the Holy Ghost" (13:52).

The phrase "speaking in [new, unknown, other or divers kinds of] tongues" is used in the Bible in reference to (1) the baptism or receiving of the Holy Spirit (Acts 2:4; 10:46; 19:6); to (2) the last two gifts of the nine gifts of the Holy Spirit (1 Corinthians 12:8-10); and to (3) individual religious devotions (1 Corinthians 14:14, 15, 28). In each case, the phrase is used in connection with a spiritual manifestation: "And they were all filled with the Holy Ghost, and began to speak with other tongues, as the Spirit gave them utterance" (Acts 2:4, baptism in the Spirit); "[b]ut the manifestation of the Spirit is given to every man to profit withal" (1 Corinthians 12:7, gift of the Spirit); and "[f]or he that speaketh in an unknown tongue speaketh not unto men, but unto God: for no man understandeth him; howbeit in the Spirit he speaketh mysteries. . . . For if I pray in an unknown tongue, my spirit prayeth" (1 Corinthians 14:2, 14, devotions in the Spirit).

It is acknowledged that there is a difference in purpose between speaking in tongues as an indication of one of the supernatural gifts of the Spirit and speaking in tongues as an initial evidence of the baptism in the Holy Ghost—and between these two and the use of unknown tongues as a means of worshiping and communicating with God in prayer, praise and singing. However, since the manifestation is, in appearance, either exactly the same or quite similar in all of these cases, and since the references in the Bible to the speaking with tongues are associated with the working of God's Spirit in the lives of His people, no great effort is made here to show a clear-cut distinction among the various purposes for speaking in tongues.

In 1 Corinthians 14, the apostle Paul, who spoke with tongues ("I thank my God, I speak with tongues more than ye all" [v. 18]), counsels the Corinthian church regarding the wise use of this spiritual gift. He gives separate instructions for its use "in the church," that is, when speaking to the Christian assembly (v. 19), and for its use in personal devotions (vv. 14, 15, 28) outside the regular instructional part of the service or at home.

Paul states that one who prophesies in or to the Christian assembly edifies the whole church, whereas "[h]e that speaketh in an unknown tongue" edifies only himself (v. 4). The apostle indicates that one who prophesies is greater than one who speaks with tongues, unless the latter can also interpret in order that the church may be edified (v. 5). He goes so far as to say that one should not speak to the church assembly in tongues when there is no interpreter present (v. 28). To speak in tongues to the brethren in an assembly (when no interpreter is present) is, according to Paul, profitless (v. 6); the same as giving an indistinct sound on a musical instrument (v. 7), like an uncertain bugle command during battle (v. 8), of no more value than speaking into the air (v. 9), meaningless to the hearer (vv. 11, 16), not instructive (v. 19), and will cause the unlearned or unbelievers to think that those whom they hear are mad (v. 23).

Speaking in tongues to the assembly of brethren where there is an interpreter, however, is equal to the gift of prophecy (v. 5), is edifying to the church (vv. 5, 12, 13, 26), and should follow this pattern: "If any man speak in an unknown tongue, let it be by two, or at the most by three, and that by course; and let one interpret" (v. 27). Paul this pattern could be followed because "the spirits of the prophets are subject to the prophets" (v. 32); and he advised to " [l]et all things be done decently and in order" (v. 40).

Paul places no great limitations, however, on the manifestation of this gift when the believer is alone and seeking spiritual edification: "He that speaketh in an unknown tongue edifieth himself" (v. 4); when the believer is in prayer and in praiseful singing: "For if I pray in an unknown tongue, my spirit prayeth, but my understanding is unfruitful. What is it then? I will pray with the spirit . . . I will sing with the spirit" (vv. 14, 15); when the believer is in church (assembly) and there is an interpreter present (v. 27); and even when the believer is in church where there is no interpreter provided he speaks inaudibly: "But if there be no interpreter, let him keep silence in the church; and let him speak to himself, and to God" (v. 28).

The apostle Paul comprehended the spiritual significance of speaking in tongues: "For he that speaketh in an unknown tongue speaketh not unto men, but unto God: for no man understandeth him; howbeit in the spirit he speaketh mysteries" (v. 2); desired that all Christians possess this gift: "I would that ye all speak with tongues" (v. 5); possessed the gift himself: "I thank my God, I speak with tongues more than ye all" (v. 18); prayed and sang in an unknown tongue (vv. 14, 15); knew that speaking in tongues was a prophesied sign from the Lord (vv. 21, 22); realized that the world would not accept it: "[A]nd yet for all that will they not hear me, saith the Lord" (v. 21); and understood that Christians were to be permitted to speak with tongues: "Wherefore, brethren, covet to prophesy, and forbid not to speak with tongues" (v. 39). Paul also knew that tongues would cease and told us when: Tongues will cease when prophecies fail, when knowledge vanishes away, and "when that which is perfect is come" (1 Corinthians 13:8-10).

The Personality of the Holy Spirit (Holy Ghost)

Both Armstrongism (The Worldwide Church of God) and the Watchtower Society (Jehovah's Witnesses) deny the personality of the Holy Ghost. In *Let God Be True*, Judge Rutherford, former leader of the Jehovah's Witnesses, defined Him as the "invisible active force of Almighty God that moves His servants to do His will." But the Bible teaches that the Holy Ghost is a divine, visible person, not some "invisible force" without personality.

Peter called the Holy Ghost *God* and said that Ananias had lied to him: "But Peter said, Ananias, why hath Satan filled thine heart to lie to the Holy Ghost. . . . [T]hou hast not lied unto men, but unto God" (Acts 5:3, 4). Could one lie to a "force" without personality? The "force" was identified as God, who is, indeed, a person.

Isaiah speaks of the Lord as having a voice, seeking to send someone with a message: "Also I heard the voice of the Lord, saying, Whom shall I send, and who will go for us? Then said I, Here am I; send me. And he said, Go, and tell this people, Hear ye indeed, but understand not; and see ye indeed, but perceive not" (Isaiah 6:8, 9). Paul identifies the same speaker as the Holy Ghost: "Well spake the Holy Ghost by Esaias the prophet unto our fathers, Saying, Go unto this people, and say, Hearing ye shall hear, and shall not understand; and seeing ye shall see, and not perceive" (Acts 28:25, 26). Can a "force" have a voice and speak messages? This "force," the Holy Ghost, was identified as the Lord (or Jehovah), who is, indeed, a person.

The Holy Spirit is a visible entity, one that has been seen:

And Jesus, when he was baptized, went up straightway out of the water: and, lo, the heavens were opened unto him, and he saw the Spirit of God descending like a dove, and lighting upon him (Matthew 3:16).

And straighway coming up out of the water, he saw the heavens opened, and the Spirit like a dove descending upon him (Mark 1:10).

And the Holy Ghost descended in a bodily shape like a dove upon him, and a voice came from heaven, which said, Thou art my beloved Son; in thee I am well pleased (Luke 3:22).

And I knew him not: but he that sent me to baptize with water, the same said unto me, Upon whom thou shalt see the Spirit descending, and remaining on him, the same is he which baptizeth with the Holy Ghost (John 1:33).

It would be difficult to see an "invisible force."

The Holy Ghost, like a person, teaches and brings things to the remembrance of the Lord's disciples: "But the Comforter, which is the Holy Ghost, whom the Father will send in my name, he shall teach you all things, and bring all things to your remembrance, whatsoever I have said unto you" (14:26). Is such possible of an impersonal "force"?

The Holy Spirit speaks, hears and shows, like a person: "Howbeit when he, the Spirit of truth, is come, he will guide you into all truth: for he shall not speak of himself;

but whatsoever he shall hear, that shall he speak: and he will shew you things to come" (16:13). Can an "invisible force," like electricity, hear?

The Holy Spirit testifies of Christ, like a person: "But when the Comforter is come, whom I will send unto you from the Father, even the Spirit of truth, which proceedeth from the Father, he shall testify of me" (15:26). Only individual beings are spoken of in Scripture as testifying about the Lord.

The Holy Spirit can be grieved like a person: "And grieve not the holy Spirit of God, whereby ye are sealed unto the day of redemption" (Ephesians 4:30). Can an atomic "force" be grieved? Does the wind, "an invisible active force," have such emotions?

The Holy Ghost can be resisted in a stubborn manner, like a person: "Ye stiffnecked and uncircumcised in heart and ears, ye do always resist the Holy Ghost: as your fathers did, so do ye" (Acts 7:51).

The Holy Ghost, like a person, calls out people (through the gift of prophecy, or probably, the gifts of tongues and interpretation), assigns them tasks, and sends them forth: "As they ministered to the Lord, and fasted, the Holy Ghost said, Separate me Barnabas and Saul for the work whereunto I have called them. . . . So they, being sent forth by the Holy Ghost, departed unto Seleucia; and from thence they sailed to Cyprus" (13:2, 4). What invisible "force" could perform such complicated actions?

The Holy Ghost can be blasphemed (openly, maliciously, deliberately proclaiming that the Lord Jesus works through the power of the devil [Mark 3:22] and that the Lord has an "unclean spirit" [v. 30]): "And the scribes which came down from Jerusalem said, He hath Beelzebub, and by the prince of the devils casteth he out devils. . . . But he that shall blaspheme against the Holy Ghost hath never forgiveness, but is in danger of eternal damnation: Because they said, He hath an unclean spirit" (vv. 22, 29, 30). Can one insult or blaspheme the "invisible force" of gravity?

NOTE: How can a person know that he is not guilty of this terrible, inexpiable sin against God's Spirit? The answer is simply that if he can still come to the Lord Jesus Christ in prayer, he is responding to a drawing of God through His Holy Spirit—and hope plentifully abounds: "No man can come to me, except the Father which hath sent me draw him: and I will raise him up at the last day" (John 6:44).

Therefore, whenever a person comes to an altar of prayer in a church in order to seek salvation through the Lord Jesus Christ, he is responding to a drawing of the Holy Ghost (John 6:44); and his case is, therefore, certainly not hopeless. Whenever a person calls upon the Lord while driving down the road, or prays in his office, or drops to his knees by his bed at night—or anywhere else at any other time—to call upon the Lord Jehovah (Acts 2:21; Romans 10:13) to save him, to help him, to heal him, to sanctify him, to fill him, to use him, or to give him grace and wisdom, he is responding to a drawing of the Spirit of God (John 6:44); and his is, therefore, in no way a hopeless case.

Since the "Lord is . . . not willing that any should perish, but that all should come to repentance" (2 Peter 3:9), He is going to work through the Holy Ghost to draw every last soul—every minute possible of every day—to the Lord Jesus Christ, the only possible means of salvation (Acts 4:12). And any response to that drawing is the absolute opposite of hopelessness (John 6:44).

Since "God our Saviour . . . will [wants to] have all men to be saved, and to come unto the knowledge of the truth" (1 Timothy 2:3, 4), He will use His Holy Spirit to draw them, every part of every day and night, to the Son of God—who came specifically "to seek and to save that which was lost" (Luke 19:10)—as long as there is the slightest hope of response to that wooing of His Spirit (John 6:44). And any feeble response, any positive reaction to the Holy Ghost's drawing is totally, completely contrary to the effect of despondency and hopelessness.

And when such seekers, responding to that drawing of God's Holy Ghost (John 6:44), come penitently to the Lord Jesus Christ in prayer, praise and/or worship (note the case of the demoniac of Gadara who was possessed [Mark 5:1-8]), they are given absolute, total, eternal assurance that God's Holy Son will never, ever refuse to accept them or ever turn them away: "[A]nd him that cometh to me I will in no wise cast out" (John 6:37). Jesus, the Christ—the Messiah, the Anointed One—was Emmanuel, the God with us (Matthew 1:23), and consequently, could not lie (Titus 1:2; Hebrews 6:18); therefore, His promise to accept those who come to Him, prayerfully and penitently, is irrevocably binding and cannot be broken.

It is important to remember that these doubts, fears and feelings of hopelessness are the products of "your adversary the devil" (1 Peter 5:8), who will often speak to the minds of people, saved or unsaved, but especially to the weak Christians, telling them that they have gone too far in sin to be saved, that they are irretrievably damned, that they have committed some unforgivable transgression,

219

and that they, consequently, can never be saved. But the devil "[and] there is no truth in him . . . is a liar, and the father of it" (John 8:44).

The Enemy will frequently accuse Christians, by speaking to their minds, of horrible sins that are most often not sins at all but simply and only his temptations. He will tempt—and frighten—people by putting in their minds the most evil kinds of thoughts.

The case of Job is a good example. After Job's multiple tragedies and great personal losses, the devil, through Job's wife, tried to induce him to blaspheme God: "Then said his wife unto him, Dost thou still retain thine integrity? curse God, and die" (Job 2:9, *NIV*). But Job, who revealed some fear of this frightful sin's occurring within his family (1:4, 5), did not give in to the temptation (2:10), even though it was in his mind and even though the Lord had permitted Satan to smite him "with sore boils from the sole of his foot unto his crown" (v. 7). The temptation— the thought in the mind—is not a sin, and certainly not the unpardonable sin. It is "when lust [the thought and temptation and desire to do it] hath conceived [that], it bringeth forth sin: and sin, when it is finished [that], bringeth forth death" (James 1:15).

Another example of great temptation is that of Jesus. The devil spoke to Him—therefore, he can speak to our minds—in an effort to cause Him to doubt His deity: "If [the big "If"] thou be the Son of God [not "Thou art the Son of God"], command this stone that it be made bread" (Luke 4:3). Note two things here: (1) The devil's attack was to tempt Him through His then greatest weakness, hunger—He had just fasted 40 days; and (2) Jesus, who of course, never sinned (1 Peter 2:22), did not obey the devil's command to turn the stone into bread—in order to prove who He was. But, over and over, the Lord Jesus used the Word—the same tool that we can use— against the devil, especially when Satan tempted Him to worship him and, then, tempted Him to "tempt the Lord [his] God"—and "the devil . . departed from him for a season" (Luke 4:13).

Although the devil, who is the thief that "cometh not, but for to steal, and to kill, and to destroy" (John 10:10), tells many of us who try to serve God that we are hopelessly lost as a result of having committed some irresistibly sinful act, we know that "[and that] there is no truth in him . . . he is [an inveterate, persistent, habitual] liar, and the father of it" (John 8:44). But the Lord Jesus Christ, who came "that [we] might have life, and that [we] might have it more abundantly," (John l0:10), gives us bountiful hope through His promise that any desire or attempt to come to Him—prayerfully, penitently, worshipfully— is a direct response to the drawing of God's Spirit (John 6:44) and, that when we come to Him, He will always accept us—in 100 percent of the cases (John 6:37). And we can indeed depend on His promise because He, Jesus, was God the Son (Hebrews 1:8; John 1:1) who could never, ever lie (Titus 1:2; Hebrews 6:18).

Those people who would be guilty of having committed that unforgivable transgression, that unpardonable sin against the Holy Spirit of God would be like those to whom Jesus spoke in the gospels (Matthew 12:22-32; Mark 3:22-30). They "came down from Jerusalem" (Mark 3:22) apparently purposefully to denounce the Lord Jesus as an imposter. Then, having seen Him perform miracles that only God could do (Mark 3:22; Matthew 12:13-15, 22), these Jewish spiritual leaders (who "held a council against him, how they might destroy him [Matthew 12:14]) knowingly, overtly, publicly, maliciously, spitefully, slanderously, hatefully, bitterly, caustically, and willfully—not innocently—proclaimed that Jesus was possessed of and worked with the devil: "He hath Beelzebub, and by the prince of devils casteth he out devils" (Mark 3:22).

And, in a maximal effort to leave absolutely no doubt about the conduct of those scribes who had come down from Jerusalem to accuse the Messiah, the Gospel of Mark very clearly—but quite succinctly—defines, or redefines, their sin: "Because they said, He hath an unclean spirit" (Mark 3:30; read also Mark 5:1-8). These scribes (in Mark 3:22), as well as the Pharisees (in Matthew 12:24), were deliberately, intentionally and openly—not ignorantly: they had seen the miracles—announcing to the public, to the world, that the Holy Ghost in Christ—the Holy Spirit, the Comforter, the Spirit of God—was "Beelzebub . . . the prince of devils" (Mark 3:22).

It is people like these who could not or would not respond to a drawing of God's Holy Spirit because they would feel or sense no conviction or reproof of sin (convicting a person of sin is a work of the Holy Ghost [John 16:8]), no desire to live righteously in Christ (causing a person to want to live righteously is a work of the Spirit of God [v. 83]), and no fear of God's judgment (putting a fear of judgment in the sinner's heart is a work of the Holy Spirit [v. 8]).

But, in summary, hope ever abounds for that earnest and penitent soul who can respond and react to that tugging of God's Holy Spirit, drawing him to Christ (John 6:44), the only possible means of salvation (Acts 4:12), and a Savior who has never yet and never will "cast out" any one "that cometh to" Him (John 6:37).

And, finally, for that Christian who may often be "weak in the faith" (Romans 14:1)—one of the favorite targets of "that old serpent, which is the Devil, and Satan" (Revelation 20:2)—who suffers the buffeting of the "messenger of Satan," as Paul did (2 Corinthians 12:7-10); who suffers the destructive onslaughts of the devil, as Job did (Job 1:7—2:10); and who suffers the temptation by the Enemy to doubt and to tempt God, as Jesus did (Luke 4:1-13), but who steadfastly witnesses for Christ, there is, again, a world of hope and assurance.

That weak Christian should always remember—when that "dragon" speaks to him and brands him as a failure as a servant of the Lord, as irredeemably lost and without God— that his faithful witnessing and testimony for Christ believe those charges and accusations of that Father of Lies (John 8:44) and are actually a means of overcoming him: "And they overcame him [the devil] by the blood of the Lamb, and by the word of their testimony" (Revelation 12:11).

The fact that he is witnessing to the lost—especially in hospitals, jails, nursing homes, prisons, and shut-in homes (Matthew 25:31-46)—telling them that Jesus is the Son of God, the Savior of lost souls, is a positive indication that Jehovah God still abides with him: "Whosoever shall confess that Jesus is the Son of God, God dwelleth in him, and he in God" (1 John 4:15).

The fact that he is lifting up Jesus as the Lord of lords and that he is preaching and declaring Christ's lordship to the lost in this world demonstrates conclusively that his faithful witnessing is an unction of and is anointed by the Holy Spirit of God: "Wherefore I give you to understand ... that no man can say that Jesus is the Lord, but by the Holy Ghost" (1 Corinthains 12:3).

And since God's Holy Ghost dwells within him, the devil and his demons cannot ever in any way possess him. Why? "[B]ecause greater is he [the Holy Spirit] that is in you, than he [Satan] that is in the world" (1 John 4:4). And, in fact, the Enemy cannot even touch or harm him (without God's permission in a trial [Job 1:6—2:1-10], which trial God will never permit to be too great for him—with God's assured help—to handle [1 Corinthians 10:13]): "We know that whosoever is born of God sinneth not; but he that is begotten of God keepeth himself, and that wicked one toucheth him not" (1 John 5:18).

NOTE: "Holy Ghost" and "Holy Spirit" are synonymous: "Ghost" derives from our Anglo-Saxon heritage (from the Anglo-Saxon word *gast*, which meant breath, spirit or soul), which had its roots in the Low German tribes (the modern German word for the Holy Ghost or Holy Spirit is *der Heilige Geist*) that invaded England in the fifth and sixth centuries.

"Spirit" derives from our Anglo-Norman heritage (from, originally, the Latin word *Spiritus*, through the Old French, or Old Norman French, word *espirit* or *esperit*), which had its roots in the Normandy French (the modern French word for the Holy Spirit or Holy Ghost is *le Saint Esprit*) that conquered England at the Battle of Hastings in 1066 and whose language, French, became the official language of the English court for some one hundred years, heavily influencing the vocabulary of even modern English.

Languages other than English, such as Spanish (*Espiritu Santo*) or French (*Saint Esprit*) or German (*Heiliger Geist*), use only one designation for the third person of the Trinity, whereas English, because of its linguistic background, developed two such titles, Holy Ghost and Holy Spirit, which have exactly the same meanings.

Using That Power to Witness for Christ

As stated earlier, the primary objective of the Lord Jesus Christ in coming into the world was soulwinning: "For the Son of man is come to seek and to save that which was lost" (Luke 19:10). And He fulfilled that objective primarily through personal evangelism: He witnessed to and won the Samaritan woman at a public well (John 4:6-39); He called the wealthy tax collector, Zacchaeus, down out of a tree on a public road through Jericho, witnessed to and won him in his home (Luke 19:1-9); and He witnessed to, delivered and won the demoniac of Gadara at a public boat landing, and, then, sent him home to witness to his family and friends (Mark 5:1-19).

In this way then the Lord Jesus gave His followers an excellent example and a good, clear-cut sense of direction for soulwinning: He witnessed to individuals on 28 occasions, whereas He preached only four sermons, a ratio of seven to one in favor of personal evangelism.

And Jesus not only set an example for soulwinning Christians, but He left them a plan for witnessing to and winning the world as well—One message for all the world: Jesus! "Neither is there salvation in any other: for there is none other name under heaven given among men, whereby we must be saved" (Acts 4:12). And all of His followers carrying that one message to the entire world: "Go ye [all of you, all of my disciples] into all the world [to all people] and preach the gospel [proclaim, witness to, tell the good news—one message] to every creature [again, to all people, to very person]" (Mark 16:15). And this one basic plan for witnessing—delivering that one simple message to the entire world—became indeed the responsibility, even unto this day, of every born-again believer.

1. *New converts.* Jesus included the spiritually new-born Christian, even before he is baptized in the Spirit—remember Apollos—in His one basic plan for all of His disciples to witness for and confess Christ: "That if thou shalt confess with thy mouth the Lord Jesus, and shalt believe in thine heart that God hath raised him from the dead, thou shalt be saved" (Romans 10:9). But can a newly converted follower of Christ become an immediate and successful witness for Christ? That same Samaritan woman at the well certainly did: "The woman then left her waterpot, and went her way into the city, and saith to the men, Come, see a man, which told me all things that ever I did: is not this the Christ? Then they went out of the city, and came unto him. . . . And many of the Samaritans of that city believed on him for the saying of the woman, which testified [witnessed], He told me all that ever I did" (John 4:28-30, 39).

Another new Christian, Andrew, successfully witnessed to and won his brother, Simon Peter, who became, in all probability, Andrew's greatest, most effective convert: "And the two disciples heard him [John the Baptist] speak, and they followed Jesus. . . . One of the two which heard John speak, and followed him, was Andrew, Simon Peter's brother. He first findeth his own brother Simon, and saith unto him, We have found the Messias, which is, being interpreted, the Christ. And he brought him to Jesus" (1:37, 40-42).

The apostle Paul, who was often imperiled by the enemy (2 Corinthians 11:23-27) and who was sorely buffeted by "the messenger of Satan" (12:7-10), implored "the saints which are at Ephesus" (Ephesians 1:1) to pray "always with all prayer and supplication in the Spirit . . . for me, that utterance may be given unto me, that I may open my mouth boldly, to make known the mystery of the gospel" (6:18, 19).

Paul's prayer was answered: He witnessed boldly, and with shattering effect, to Felix, the Roman governor of Judea: "[Felix] sent for Paul, and heard him concerning the faith in Christ. And as he [Paul] reasoned of righteousness, temperance, and judgment to come Felix trembled, and answered, Go thy way for this time; when I have a convenient season, I will call for thee" (Acts 24:24, 25).

His bold overcoming testimony to Herod Agrippa had an equally impressive effect on that king and leader: "King Agrippa, believest thou the prophets? I know that thou believest. Then Agrippa said unto Paul, Almost thou persuadest me to be a Christian" (26:27, 28).

And Paul's final testimony—the testimony of a Christian who had known and suffered the most serious onslaughts and oppressions of the devil—echoed his victory over that evil one through his constantly bold preaching, testimony and witnessing for Christ: "Nothwithstanding the Lord stood with me, and strengthened me; that by me the preaching might be fully known, and that all the Gentiles might hear: and I was delivered out of the mouth of the lion. And the Lord shall deliver me from every evil work, and will preserve me unto his heavenly kingdom: to whom be glory forever and ever. . . . Henceforth there is laid up for me a crown of righteousness, which the Lord, the righteous judge, shall give me at that day: and not to me only, but to all them also that love his appearing" (2 Timothy 4:17, 18, 8).

2. *Witnessing for Christ.* The Christian who has been filled with the Holy Ghost has an irrevocable command and "great power" to evangelize one on one: "But ye shall receive power, after that the Holy Ghost is come upon you: and ye shall be witnesses unto me both in Jerusalem, and in all Judaea, and in Samaria, and unto the uttermost part of the earth" (Acts 1:8).

The apostle Peter, "filled with the Holy Ghost" (4:8) and in obedience to Christ's command (1:8), testified boldly, powerfully to the Jewish "rulers, and elders, and scribes" (4:5) that "Neither is there salvation in any other: for there is none other name under heaven given among men, whereby we must be saved" (4:12).

Peter and John, released from incarceration, returned and reported "to their own company" (v. 23), after which the group worshiped and praised God and then prayed (4:23-31); and "the place was shaken where they were assembled together; and they were all filled with the Holy Ghost, and they spake the word of God with boldness" (v. 31). "And with great power gave the apostles witness of the resurrection of the Lord Jesus" (v. 33); and many "believed" and were saved (v. 32).

3. *One message for all.* It is quite simple for one to be saved; Paul said as much to the Corinthian Christians: "But I fear, lest by any means, as the serpent beguiled Eve through his subtilty, so your minds should be corrupted from the simplicity that is in Christ" (2 Corinthains 11:3). How simple is it to be saved? Again it is Paul, quoting Joel 2:32 (who was also quoted by Peter in Acts 2:21), who reveals the simplicty that is in Christ's salvation: "For whosoever shall call upon the name of the Lord shall be saved" (Romans 10:13).

It was simple for the thief on the cross to be saved: "And he said unto Jesus, Lord, remember me when thou comest into thy kingdom. And Jesus said unto him, Verily I say unto thee, To day shalt thou be with me in paradise" (Luke 23:42, 43).

It was simple for the woman caught in adultery to be saved: "[Jesus] said unto her, Woman where are those thine accusers? hath no man condemned thee? She said, No man, Lord. And Jesus said unto her, Neither do I condemn thee: go, and sin no more" (John 8:10, 11).

It was simple for the publican praying in the temple to be saved: "And the publican, standing afar off, would not lift up so much as his eyes unto heaven, but smote upon his breast, saying, God be merciful to me a sinner. I tell you, this man went down to his house justified" (Luke 18:13, 14).

It was simple for the Ethiopian eunuch to be saved: "And Philip said, If thou believest with all thine heart, thou mayest. And he answered and said, I believe that Jesus Christ is the Son of God. And he commanded the chariot to stand still: and they went down both into the water, both Philip and the eunuch; and he baptized him" (Acts 8:37, 38).

It is a simple thing to be saved; the difficulties arise in the battles and struggles to overcome the world and to grow in grace. And even these latter problems are made easier for the Christian who remembers to cast every one of his cares, anxieties, burdens and problems on the Lord: "Casting all [all, all, all] your care upon him; for he careth for you" (1 Peter 5:7).

The one simple message of salvation for all or the one simple step to salvation for all involves four actions on the part of the sinner: He must (1) believe that Christ Jesus was the Son of God ("Believe on the Lord Jesus Christ, and thou shalt be saved" [Acts 16:31]); he must (2) confess his sins ("If we confess our sins, he is faithful and just to forgive us *our* sins, and to cleanse us from all unrighteousness" [John 1:93]); he must (3) repent of and, with God's help, turn from his sins ("I [Jesus] tell you, Nay: but, except ye repent, ye shall all likewise perish" [Luke 13:3]); and he must (4) confess (witness for) Christ as a resultant phase of salvation ("That if thou shalt confess with thy mouth the Lord Jesus, and shalt believe in thine heart that God hath raised him from the dead, thou shalt be saved" [Romans 10:9]).

Dr. D. James Kennedy's Evangelism Explosion witnessing program offers the most effective presentation of the one simple gospel message for witnessing to the unsaved that has been developed in this century. Herewith follows an explanation of the gospel of Christ that is based on Dr. Kennedy's excellent gospel presentation. If the person who desires to be an effective witness and a productive soulwinner will study, learn and internalize this one-message material, he will "*be* ready always to *give* an answer to every man that asketh [him] a reason of the hope that is in [him]" (1 Peter 3:15).

4. *Eternal life!* Free! Absolutely free! Eternal life is free! It costs you nothing; it is neither earned nor merited; it is not the result of works ("Not by works of righteousness [Titus 3:5]"; "Not by works, lest any man should boast" [Ephesians 2:9]). Eternal life is a gift—a free gift, an entirely unearned gift of God: "[T]he gift of God *is* eternal life through Jesus Christ our Lord" (Romans 6:23).

Isn't that exciting news? Eternal life, forever in heaven, costs neither a penny of your money nor an hour of your labor! You do not have to pay your way or work your way into heaven.

A simple question emphasizes the importance of being certain that one possesses this free eternal life: Have you arrived at that place in your spiritual life where you are sure that, if you were to die tonight, you would go to heaven?

Often the response to this question is: "I don't think anyone could know that for sure!"

But the Bible tells us that one can know for sure. As a matter of fact, John says that the Word of God was written specifically so that one may know that he has eternal life: "These things have I written . . . that ye may know that ye have eternal life" (1 John 5:13).

The answer to a second simple question focuses on whether one does or does not have this free gift of eternal life and focuses on the way to receive it: What if you were to die tonight, were to stand before God and He were to ask you, "Why should I permit you to enter My Heaven?" What would your answer be? That's not an easy question, is it?

If you are uncertain as to your answer to this second question, I believe that I have, specifically for you, the greatest news that you have ever heard. Now that is saying a whole lot, isn't it? But I think that I can substantiate it.

First, let me repeat that heaven, or salvation or eternal life, is a free gift: "For the wages of sin is death; but the gift of God *is* eternal life through Jesus Christ our Lord" (Romans 6:23). If salvation is a gift, an absolutely free gift, then it is neither earned nor deserved: "Not by works of righteousness which we have done, but according to his mercy he saved us" (Titus 3:5); "For by grace [the unmerited favor of God] are ye saved through faith [believing in and trusting Christ alone for one's eternal salvation]; and that not of yourselves: it is the gift of God: Not of works [which are only an outward result or showing or evidence of an inward faith (James 2:17, 18)], lest any man should boast" (Ephesians 2:8, 9).

Second, the Bible teaches that all human beings have sinned ("For all have sinned, and come short of the glory of God" [Romans 3:23]), are unrighteous ("As it is written, There is none righteous, no, not one" [v. 10]), and, unless they accept God's free gift of eternal life, will receive the wages of sin ("For the wages of sin is death" [6:23]), which "death" is eternal separation from God in the "lake of fire" ("This is the second death" [Revelation 20:14]), "where the beast [a "man" according to Revelation 13:18 and 2 Thessalonians 2:3] and the false prophet [another man] *are*, and shall be tormented day and night for ever and ever" (Revelation 20:10).

That could sound discouraging, especially since God commands that we be perfect and since the Bible says that we "all have sinned" (Romans 3:28) and that "[t]here is none righteous, no, not one" (v. 10).

But do not be discouraged, for there is a super abundance of hope; and that hope starts with God.

Therefore, the third point is that "God is love" (1 John 4:8) and does not want to punish us: "The Lord . . . is longsuffering to us-ward, not willing that any should perish [be lost, unsaved, without eternal life], but that all should come to repentance [turn from their sins]" (2 Peter 3:9). But God is just; therefore, if we do not "come to repentance" and "believe on the Lord Jesus Christ" (Acts 16:31), He must punish us: "Except ye repent [turn from sin], ye shall all likewise perish" (Luke 13:3). But God required the sacrifice of a sinless man whose blood would cleanse us from sin and prevent our perishing.

Point four says: God the Son ("the Word" [John 1:1]), the second person of the divine Trinity, solved this latter problem in the most amazing way by entering into the world in the person of Jesus Christ (who is called *God* in Matthew 1:22, 23 ["God with us"]; in John 20:28 ["My Lord and my God"]; in Isaiah 9:6 ["The mighty God"]; in John 1:1 ["the Word was God"]; in Hebrews 1:8 ["Thy throne, O God, is for ever"]) who died on the cross and shed His blood for our sins:

"[T]he blood of Jesus Christ his Son cleanseth us from all sin" (1 John 1:7). He died, sacrificed Himself, to pay for our sins and arose and is alive, again, to show that He purchased a place in heaven for us, which He offers as a gift, a free gift, a gift which costs nothing: "[T]he gift of God is eternal life [in heaven] through Jesus Christ our Lord" (Romans 6:23).

And, fifth, this free gift is received by faith: "For by grace [God's unmerited favor] are ye saved through faith [belief or trust in Christ (Acts 16:31)]; and that not of yourselves: *it is* the [free] gift of God" (Ephesians 2:8). Faith is not mere intellectual assent but a simple trust in Jesus Christ—and in Him alone—for salvation, the free gift of eternal life: "Believe on the Lord Jesus Christ, and thou shalt be saved" (Acts 16:31).

Sixth: What steps must one take in order to receive this free gift of eternal life?

1. *Believe.* "Whosoever believeth that Jesus is the Christ [the Messiah, the Anointed One] is born of God" (1 John 5:1). One is saved by believing "on the Lord Jesus Christ" (Acts 16:31). He alone bore all of our sins (1 Peter 2:24; Isaiah 53:6); and no religion, church organization, ritual, temple or individual—other than Jesus—can in any way save lost men: "Neither is there salvation in any other: for there is none other name under heaven given among men, whereby we must be saved" (Acts 4:12).

2. *Confessing sins.* "If we confess our sins, he is faithful and just to forgive us our sins, and to cleanse us from all unrighteousness" (1 John 1:9); "God be merciful to me a sinner. . . . this man went down to his house justified" (Luke 18:13, 14). Since Jesus bore all of our sins and iniquities (Isaiah 53:6), since no sacrifice other than that of Christ will remove our sins (Hebrews 10:4), since Christ's sacrificial offering is sufficient for the cleansing of everyone (Hebrews 10:10), since "works of righteousness" will not save us (Titus 3:5), then all that God initially demands of a sinner is the acknowledgement of his sinfulness and a confession of his sins.

3. *Turning from sin.* "I [Jesus] tell you, Nay: but, except ye repent, ye shall all likewise perish" (Luke 13:3). Accompanying one's confession of sins must be a willingness, with God's help, to forsake sin and to change one's attitude toward sin and his love for it. Repentance is a condition demanded of the sinner by God in order that his sins "may be blotted out" (Acts 3:19).

234

4. *Confessing Christ as a resultant phase of salvation.* That if thou shalt confess with thy mouth the Lord Jesus, and shalt believe in thine heart that God hath raised him from the dead, thou shalt be saved. For with the heart man believeth unto righteousness; and with the mouth confession is made unto salvation" (Romans 10:9, 10).

If the person to whom you are witnessing has not received eternal life, encourage him or her to take the first steps of this process by merely talking directly and sincerely to the Lord in this simple prayer of salvation: "Lord Jesus, I want You to come into my life right now. I am a sinner. I have been trusting in myself and my own works. But now I put my trust in You. I accept You as my own personal Savior. I believe that You died for me. I receive You as my Lord and Master over my life. Help me to turn from my sins and to follow You. I accept Your gift of eternal life. I am not worthy of it, but I thank You for it. And I thank You for sending Your Holy Spirit into my life and for letting me be born again. Amen."

Have the new convert fill out the following decision card. Tear off the bottom portion and give it to him or her as a means of follow-up instructions. Give the top portion to the follow-up secretary. Get the new convert into a discipling class, possibly on Sunday mornings, as soon as practicable so that—through Bible study, worship services, daily prayer and regular witnessing—he or she can experience healthy spiritual growth in God's grace, especially and specifically to avoid backsliding.

DECISION CARD

I prayed the sinner's prayer, confessing and repenting of my sins and believing on and trusting Christ alone for my salvation. I know that this means that He forgave me, and that He came into my life, and that I now have the free gift of eternal life.

NAME_____

AGE_____ TELEPHONE_____

ADDRESS_____

CITY_____

STATE_____ ZIP_____

NOTE: If you prayed the commitment prayer—and, thus, received eternal life—you should continue to "walk in the light" (1 John 1:7) by (1) being baptized (Matthew 28:19), (2) praying daily (1 Thessalonians 5:17), (3) reading and studying God's Word regularly (2 Timothy 2:15), (4) attending Sunday school and/or church worship services (Hebrews 10:25), (5) giving to the cause of Christ (Malachi 3:8-10), (6) praying for power to witness for Christ (Acts 1:8; 2:4; 8:17; 10:44-46; 19:6), (7) confessing (witnessing) to the world and to the lost that Jesus is the Savior, the Son of God (1 John 4:15; Romans 10:9, 10; Acts 1:8; Revelation 12:11), and (8) by developing in your life the fruit of the Spirit (Galatians 5: 22, 23).

5. *Witnessing to cultists.* A cult is a group of people following, usually, one leader and that leader's own, private interpretation of the Scriptures, in which interpretation he customarily denies one or more of six major historical doctrines of Christianity: the deity of Christ, the Trinity, the personality of the Holy Ghost, the bodily resurrection in one phase or another, the physical return of Christ after the tribulation, and eternal punishment for the unsaved.

Therefore, one or more of these extremely important Biblical doctrines normally must be dealt with first before the cultist will usually listen to the "one message." The experienced cultist, especially the Jehovah's Witness or the Mormon, has heard bits and pieces of the "one message;" but he or she is uninfluenced by the Christian's witness and testimony because he or she has been taught repeatedly that (1) his or her religion is the only true religion, that (2) all other religions are of the devil, and that (3) Christians have incorrectly interpreted Biblical doctrines.

The reason for dealing very thoroughly and Biblically with one of the listed doctrines denied by cultists is to shake and, therefore, weaken the cultists' faith in the error-ridden theology and the inaccurate Biblical interpretations of their mind-controlling, brainwashing parent religious organization. Once the sincere cultist begins to comprehend the errors that he or she has been taught, once he sees that he has been deliberately and greatly deceived, then the Christian witness can open his Bible and begin, verse by verse, to explain to the cultist the simple Biblical plan of God's salvation, the "one message for all."

6. *Pre-witnessing to the Jehovah's Witnesses.* The most effective method of pre-witnessing to cultists is to ask questions that the average cultist cannot explain, especially questions on the errors in his basic doctrines. The erroneous teaching of who Jesus really is is the starting point for pre-witnessing to Jehovah's Witnesses.

One of the major teachings of the Watchtower Bible and Tract Society (Jehovah's Witnesses) is that Jesus is not deity, that He is not God as the Father is God, that Jesus is not equal to the Father: "Christ is God's Son and is inferior to him." "Christ was [the] first of God's creations,"

237

(*Jehovah's Witnesses in the Twentieth Century*, rev. ed. [Watchtower Bible and Tract Society: New York, 1979], p. 13). "The justice of God would not permit that Jesus, as a ransom, be *more* than a perfect man; and certainly not be the supreme God Almighty in the flesh." "If Jesus was God, then during Jesus' death God was dead and in the grave." "If Jehovah and the dead Christ were one in substance, the resurrection would have been impossible," (J.F. Rutherford, *Let God Be True* [Watchtower Bible and Tract Society: New York, 1946], pp. 88, 91, 92).

Ask the Jehovah's Witness: If Jesus is not "Mighty God," equal to Jehovah who is called "Mighty God" in the *New World Translation*, Isaiah 10:20, 21, and "the mighty One" in Jeremiah 32:18, (*NWT*) then how do you explain Isaiah 9:6 (*NWT*), which prophesies the birth of Christ and calls Him "Mighty God"? Have the Jehovah's Witnesses read also Matthew 28:18 in which Jesus claims (in the KJV) to have been given "all power" in heaven and in earth. "All powerful" and "almighty" are synonymous.

Ask the Jehovah's Witness: If Jesus is not "God with us," how do you explain Matthew 1:22, 23? Have him read and explain the verses.

Ask the Jehovah's Witness: If Jesus is not God, how do you explain John 20:28? Have him read and explain the verse. Ask the Jehovah's Witness: If Jesus is not God, how do you explain John 1:1 in the *Kingdom Interlinear Translation*, on the left side of page 417, where it says that "God was the Word?" Have him read and explain the verse.

Ask the Jehovah's Witness: If Jesus is not God, how do you explain Hebrews 1:8 in the *Kingdom Interlinear Translation*, on the left side of page 965, where it says that the Father calls the Son God: "The throne of you the

God [is] into the age of the age?" Have him read and explain the verse.

Ask the Jehovah's Witness: If Jesus does not have "all the fulness of the Godship [God head]," how do you explain Colossians 2:9 in the *Kingdom Interlinear Translation*, on the left side of page 899? Have him read and explain the verse.

Ask the Jehovah's Witness: If Jesus is not God, how do you explain Philippians 2:6, which says that Jesus existed in the form of God (and was therefore God just as the Jehovah's Witness exists in the form of man and is therefore man)? Have him read and explain the verse.

Show the Jehovah's Witnesses the two Jehovahs (two-thirds of the Trinity) in Genesis 19:24 (*NWT*), one Jehovah on the earth calling down sulphur and fire from Jehovah in the heavens. Have him read Jeremiah 23:5, 6, (*NWT*) where Jehovah calls Jesus (the "righteous sprout" of David) "Jehovah our Righteousness." Have him read Acts 28:25, 26 in the *New World Translation*, where Paul quotes the "holy spirit" speaking through Isaiah. In Isaiah, however, it is Jehovah who spoke (Isaiah 6:8, *NWT*), making the Holy Spirit Jehovah just as the Father and Son are called Jehovah.

NOTE: The *Kingdom Interlinear* and *New World Translations* are Watchtower Bibles that can be—and should be—purchased at a Kingdom Hall for more effectively witnessing to Jehovah's Witnesses.

7. *Pre-witnessing to Mormons.* The *Book of Mormon* contains, according to standard Mormon texts, the "fulness of the everlasting gospel" (*Doctrine and Covenants*, 27:5), the "fulness of the gospel of Jesus Christ" (*Doctrine*

and Covenants, 20:9), the "fulness of the everlasting gospel" (*Pearl of Great Price*, Joseph Smith 2:34) and is the principal and basic book of Mormonism. If it contains the fulness of the gospel of Jesus, then it should teach what Mormonism teaches; however, the *Book of Mormon* does not teach one single major doctrine of Mormonism, except water baptism, and, in fact, opposes many of Mormonism's favorite teachings.

Ask the Mormon: Do you subscribe to the teachings of Mormonism?

- *Is God flesh and bone instead of spirit?* (See Alma 22:9, 10; 31:15; John 4:24; 2 Corinthians 3:17). Note especially Alma 18:28: "And Amon said: This is God. And Ammon said unto him again: Believest thou that this Great Spirit, who is God, created all things which are in heaven and in the earth?"

- *Is there a plurality of Gods?* (See Mormon 7:7; 1 John 5:7; 1 Timothy 2:5). Note especially Alma 11:28, 29: "Now Zeezrom said: Is there more than one God? And he answered, No."

- *Is God an exalted man?* (See Hosea 11:9; Numbers 23:19; Romans 1: 22, 23). (See also Genesis 3:5; 2 Thessalonians 2:3, 4). Note especially Mosiah 8:16: "And Ammon said that a seer is a revelator and a prophet also; and a gift which is greater can no man have; except he should possess the power of God, which no man can [no man can have the power of God]; yet a man may have great power given him from God."

- *Does God change and progress?* (See Mormon 9:9, 10, 19; Malachi 3:6; James 1:17; Hebrews 13:8).

Note especially Moroni 8:18: "For I know that God is not a partial God, neither a changeable being; but he is unchangeable from all eternity to all eternity."

- *Is God married and a polygamist?* (See Jacob 2:24, 27). Note especially Jacob 1:15: "And now it came to pass that the people of Nephi, under the reign of the second king, began to grow hard in their hearts, and indulge themselves somewhat in wicked practices, such as like unto David of old desiring many wives and concubines, and also Solomon, his son."

A Mormon with any knowledge of what his church, the Church of Jesus Christ of Latter-day Saints, teaches will or should answer, "Yes," to each of these questions; however, the Book of Mormon, which is the only text listed in the Mormon "Articles of Faith" as being the correctly translated "Word of God," does not teach any of the above basic doctrines of the Mormon Church.

Now, ask the Mormon: Could you show me your teachings about your concept of God in your book, the *Book of Mormon*, which is called, in the *Doctrine and Covenants* and in the *Pearl of Great Price*, the everlasting gospel or the fulness of the gospel of the Lord Jesus Christ? If he cannot find them in the *Book of Mormon*—and they are not in that book—tell him to go home and look them up and come back next week and show them to you. Tell him that you will check with him by phone, or will come to his house, or will come by his business or place of work so that he can show you these Mormon teachings in the *Book of Mormon*. Give him your testimony and ask him if he has been born again according to Alma 5:14 or Mosiah 27:24.

Ask the Mormon also to show you in the *Book of Mormon* the Latter-day Saint teaching that (1) Jesus was not conceived by the Holy Ghost (*Journal of Discourses* 1:50, 51; see Alma 7:10), (2) Jesus is a spirit brother of Lucifer, the devil (Milton Hunter, *The Gospel Through the Ages*, p. 15), (3) the living can be baptized for the dead (see Alma 34:34, 35), (4) we preexisted as spirits, (5) the Lord Jesus was married and was a polygamist, and (6) that the priesthood is necessary for the church today (see Matthew 21:15, 27; 26:3, 4; 14, 16, 59; 27:12; 20, 41, 42, for Christ's relations with the priests).

NOTE: The *Book of Mormon* can usually be obtained through Mormon missionaries or through their church, the Church of Jesus Christ of Latter-day Saints.

8. *Pre-witnessing to Moonies.* One of the major covert teachings of Sun Myung Moon is that he, Moon, is the Lord of the Second Advent; therefore, Jesus, who failed in His mission, is now in the spirit world and will not be returning (His second advent) in the clouds. Since Moon was born, about 1920, on the earth and in the flesh, he has to discredit scriptures that teach that Christ will return in the clouds, the heavens, the air. Moon writes in the *Divine Principle* (pp. 502, 503):

Jesus was actually born in the flesh on earth, and we are compelled by this knowledge to study the Bible from the viewpoint that the Lord may come again in a like manner. . . . Jesus, who knew he was in such a situation, anticipated that if, at the Second Advent, the Lord is born as a man and appears like a thief to the Christians, who, waiting for the Messiah, would be looking at the sky alone, just as the Jews did at the coming of Jesus, the Son of man would again be condemned as a heretic and suffer many trials. Therefore, Jesus said that the Lord would be rejected by that generation. Accordingly, we must

242

know that this Biblical verse would only be fulfilled when Christ would come again in the flesh, and never if he should come on the clouds.

Ask the Moonie (follower of Sun Myung Moon): If Jesus is not coming back in the clouds of heaven, how do you explain Matthew 24:30? Have him read the verse and explain it.

Ask the Moonie: If Jesus is not "coming in a cloud," how do you explain Luke 21:27? Have him read and explain the verse.

Ask the Moonie: If the Lord Jesus Christ is not returning "in like manner as ye have seen him go into heaven," how do you explain Acts 1:9-11? Have him read and explain the verses.

Ask the Moonie: If Jesus is not going to be "revealed from heaven with his mighty angels" at the second advent, how do you explain 2 Thessalonians 1:7? Have him read and explain the verse.

Ask the Moonie: If the Lord is not coming back "with clouds" at His second advent, how do you explain Revelation 1:7? Have him read and explain the verse.

Ask the Moonie: If the second advent of the Lord has already occurred in the birth of Sun Myung Moon, how do you explain Matthew 24:29, 30, which says that His second coming (not the rapture, at which time He does not come to the earth) is "immediately after the tribulation," which is yet to occur in the future? Have him read and explain these verses.

Ask the Moonie: If the second advent has already occurred in the birth of Sun Myung Moon in Korea in 1920, how do you explain Mark 13:24-26 which says that His coming is "after the tribulation," which is yet to occur in the future? Have him read and explain these verses.

Ask the Moonie: Where does the Bible say that the Second Advent of the Lord will be in a fleshly form? Where does it say that His coming "in the clouds" is symbolic?

NOTE: Sun Myung Moon's *Divine Principle*, the Moonies' "Bible," is often difficult to obtain; however, contacts with HSA-UWC, 4 West 43rd Street, New York, NY 10036, might bring results.

9. *Pre-witnessing to Saturday Sabbatarians.* The Seventh-Day Adventists and most other Saturday Sabbatarians are not full-blown cultists (Herbert W. Armstrong's Worldwide Church of God is, however, an exception and is, therefore, a cult), because they do not absolutely deny most of the historical doctrines of Christianity—the deity of Christ, the Trinity, the personality of the Holy Spirit—however, their emphasis on keeping a part of the law and commandments of Moses (the fourth commandment)—which creates a serious problem, because it obscures Christ as the only and sufficient means of salvation (Acts 4:12)—and, especially, the Seventh-Day Adventists' rejection of the doctrine of eternal punishment for the wicked, place them in a spiritually precarious position.

A Saturday Sabbatarian is one who keeps the seventh day of the week, Saturday, as a holy day in conformity with the letter of the law as prescribed in the fourth commandment. The word *sabbath* derives from the Hebrew word *shabbath*, which means "rest" and not Saturday or seventh day.

Ask the Saturday Sabbatarian: If the seventh-day Saturday Sabbath is so important to Christians . . .

- Why did Jesus break the Sabbath (John 5:18)? Have him read the scripture and note that it was John and not the Jews who stated that He broke the Sabbath. Ask him to explain the verse.

- Why was the commandment given only to the Jews (Deuteronomy 5:15)? Have him read and explain the verse. Have him read also Acts 15:23-29 where the instructions to the Gentiles (v. 23), whose souls were being subverted by Jews who were trying to get the Gentiles to keep the law (verse 24), do not include the keeping of any holy day.

- Why was the Sabbath sometimes on the first and eighth days of the week (Leviticus 23:39)? Have him read and explain the verse. Have him read also Leviticus 25:4, which commands a Sabbath of rest for an entire year and 2 Chronicles 36:21, which speaks of a Sabbath of seventy years.

- Why was the "law of commandments," which included the Ten Commandments, abolished (Ephesians 2:15)? Have him read and explain the verse, especially in connection with Exodus 34:28 and Exodus 24:12. Have him read also Hosea 2:11, which predicts that Sabbaths would cease, and Colossians 2:14, which states that the "handwriting of ordinances"—Moses wrote the law and commandments by hand—were blotted out and nailed to the cross.

- Why does the New Testament permit a choice of days (Romans 14:5)? Have him read and explain the verse. Have him read also Colossians 2: 16, 17 and Galatians 4:9-11.

Ask also: Why did Jesus rise on Sunday (Mark 16:9), appear thrice on Sunday to His disciples (John 20:1 and 14, 19, 26), pour out the Holy Ghost on Sunday (Acts 2:1, 4; Leviticus 23:15-21), and give the Revelation on Sunday (Revelation 1:10)? And why did the disciples break bread on Sunday (Acts 20:7; 1 Corinthians 16:2)? Why do not Seventh-Day Adventists or Sabbatarians really keep the strict Sabbath (Deuteronomy 5:12-15) and when do they stone Sabbath breakers (Exodus 31:14)? Why are all of the commandments except the fourth repeated in the New Testament? The first is repeated in Matthew 22:37, the second in 1 John 5:21, the third in Colossians 3:8, the fifth in Ephesians 6:2, the 3, and the sixth through the tenth in Romans 13:8-10.

10. *Back to the message.* If the Christian witness can ever, by asking these preceding questions, get the cultist to think seriously about the destiny of his eternal soul, to question his unbased doctrines, and to investigate thoroughly his erroneous teachings in the light of God's Word, it is then possible to win him to the Lord; otherwise, it is much, much more difficult.

Pray daily for the cultists whom you are trying to win to Christ. As the opportunity arises, keep posing the difficult questions. Get him or her into the Bible, reading first the Acts of the Apostles, followed by the Gospel of John. Then, when God opens the door, present to that cultist, as effectively and as wisely as possible, the simple plan of God's salvation, that "one message for all."

11. *The effects of the message.* All of the hosts of heaven are eagerly awaiting that first or that next soul that you

will win to Christ. The world will not be aware of your witnessing success. The country in which you live will certainly not take note of your new convert. Neither will your home town or your city realize the value of your soulwinning effort. But the angels throughout this endless universe will fill the heavens with rejoicing over your great, your tremendous spiritual victory. Jesus said that they would: "Likewise, I say unto you, there is joy in the presence of the angels of God over one sinner that repenteth" (Luke 15:10).

Why? Because that one penitent soul is of greater value than this entire sin-ridden world: "For what shall it profit a man, if he shall gain the whole world, and lose his own soul?" (Mark 8:36).

You literally hold people's eternal destiny in your hands! Your witness to the lost can mean the difference between eternity in a devil's hell or eternity in God's heaven. And for some people your witnessing will be the only sure opportunity that they will ever have to find Christ as their personal Savior. God may have assigned no one else but you to the task of presenting to them the gospel message.

Pray earnestly and daily for an open door to witness, for a divine appointment to lead an eternal soul to Jesus!

The "uttermost part of the earth" has not yet been reached with the glorious gospel of Christ; "every creature" has not yet been told that Jesus alone saves from sin and hell! God needs powerful witnesses to carry out this task in these last days! Offer yourself as a witness and God will supply the power through His Holy Spirit! "Have ye received the Holy Ghost since ye believed?" (Acts 19:2).

⚡ PART THREE ⚡

BIBLE STUDY

BIBLE STUDY FOR ADULTS

Lesson 1
The Way of Salvation

MEMORIZE: Acts 16:31

To accept Jesus Christ, the promised Messiah, as your personal Savior is the most important decision of your lifetime. This means that you have been born again from above, (John 3:3). This new birth, of the Spirit of God, has made you a "new creature," (2 Corinthians 5:17). Your old beliefs, your old ideas, your old attitudes are beginning to pass away. Your whole outlook on life is becoming new, is changing. Life to you is taking on a new meaning. You now see your friends, your family, your convictions, your beliefs differently—in a new light. This newness of life is the result of your having been born again, a spiritual birth which has made you a partaker of the nature of God.

It is now necessary that you understand more thoroughly God's plan of redemption in order to be able to explain clearly this way of salvation to others who are lost in sin, so that they too may be ransomed from eternal punishment through the sacrifice of God's Son. Read the following questions; look up the Scripture references given; and, in your own words, write the answers in the spaces provided.

I. NEED OF SALVATION

A. Who has sinned (Romans 3:23)?

B. Who is the father of sinners and of sin (John 8:44; 1 John 3:8)?

C. What happens to a person who has sinned (Exodus 32:33)?

D. What will eventually happen to a person whose name is blotted out of the Book of Life (Revelation 20:15)?

II. WRONG WAYS OF SALVATION

A. Can a person be saved by doing good works (Titus 3:5)?

B. Can a person be saved by keeping the law of Moses (including the Ten Commandments) (Galatians 2:16; James 2:10)?

C. Can a person be saved by sincerely relying on his own ideas with regard to the way of salvation (Proverbs 14:12)?

III. RIGHT WAY OF SALVATION

A. How can a person desiring salvation reach God (John 14:6)?

B. Whose sins did Christ bear in His body on the cross (1 Peter 2:24)?

C. For what reason did Jesus suffer for your sins and mine (1 Peter 3:18)?

D. Why was it absolutely necessary that Jesus, instead of some other man, bear our sins (2 Corinthians 5:21)?

E. Give two reasons: (1) God's feeling toward man and (2) man's condition, why God sent Christ to die for our sins (John 3:16).

IV. MAN'S PART IN SALVATION

A. What is the first great step in a person's being saved (Acts 16:31)?

B. In the second step: (1) What must we do about our sins (1 John 1:9)? (2) What will the Lord then do with respect to our sins?

C. In man's next step toward salvation, what will happen to him if he does not turn from and give up his sins (Luke 13:3)?

D. In the last step, what does witnessing for Jesus and confessing Him as Lord indicate (Romans 10:9)?

V. TIME FOR SALVATION

A. What day is the best for a person to be saved (2 Corinthians 6:2)?

B. Why should a person not put off salvation until tomorrow (Proverbs 27:1)?

VI. VALUE OF SALVATION

A. How would you estimate the value of a soul (Mark 8:37, 38)?

B. What material blessings are promised, by the Lord, to Christians which are not promised to the unsaved (heathen, Gentiles) (Matthew 6:31-33)?

VII. SUMMARY OF THE WAYS OF SALVATION

A. What are the names of each individual (including the disciples, relatives, and parents of Christ) and each church organization (past or present) whereby a person can be saved (Acts 4:12).

Review Acts 16:31, close your Bible, and write the verse from memory.

Between now and the time you receive Lesson II, read Acts 1–7. Reading at the rate of at least one chapter per day, you will normally be able to finish the suggested number between lessons. If you read with greater than average speed and if you complete the reading of the Book of Acts before receiving the next lesson, then read chapters 1—5 of the Gospel of John.

Every Christian who desires to be a fruitful servant of the Savior, Jesus of Nazareth, should, if at all possible, do these things: Be baptized, read the Bible daily, pray daily, publicly confess and witness for Christ, attend church worship services and pay tithes.

Lesson 2
The Separated Life

I have read chapters 1—7 of the Book of Acts:
Yes ____ No ____
I have read chapters 1—5 of the Gospel of John:
Yes ____ No____

MEMORIZE: 1 John 1:9.

You have successfully completed your first lesson on "The Way of Salvation." In order to be a living witness for Christ, your life as well as your speech must be exemplary. You are to live a sanctified life, separated from the world of sin. Christ did not take you out but rather sent you into the world to serve Him (John 17:15-18); however, you, like Christ, are not of this world of sin (John 17:16). John, the beloved disciple, said, "Love not the world, neither the things that are in the world. If any man love the world, the love of the Father is not in him," (1 John 2:15).

This lesson teaches the sanctification of the believer and of his living a life apart from sin. Read the following questions; look up the Scripture references given; and, in your own words, write the answers in the space provided.

1. Is it possible for a person to serve both Christ and the world (Matthew 6:24; 12:33; 1 Corinthians 10:21)?

2. If a person serves Christ, does he have to be separated from the world (John 15:19; 2 Corinthians 6:14)? Why? (James 4:4)

3. If one serves Christ, is he to continue in sin (Romans 6:1-23; 1 Corinthians 15:34; Galatians 2:17)?

4. What four names did Peter give to those who are separated from the world for the purpose of rendering service and praise to Christ (1 Peter 2:9)?

5. What two books of the Bible were addressed to a sanctified or separated people (1 Corinthians 1:2; Jude 1)?

6. Who suffered that we might be sanctified or separated from the world (Hebrews 13:12)?

7. Did Christ pray for our sanctification (John 17:17-21)?

8. Is it God's will for us to be a sanctified or separated people (1 Thessalonians 4:3, 4)?

9. What kind of church does Christ want to present to Himself (Ephesians 5:25-27)?

10. Can we be crucified to the world and the world to us (Galatians 6:14; 2:20)?

11. What kind of vessel can Christ use (2 Timothy 2:21)?

12. Read 1 Thessalonians 5:23 as our message to you.

Review, separately, Acts 16:31 and 1 John 1:9; close your Bible; then, from memory, recite these verses.

Between now and the time you receive Lesson 3, read Acts 8-14. Reading at the rate of at least one chapter per day, you will normally be able to finish the suggested number between lessons. If you read with greater than average speed and if you complete the reading in the Book of Acts before receiving the next lesson, then read John 6-10.

Every Christian who desires to be a fruitful servant of the Savior, Jesus of Nazareth, should, if at all possible, do these things: Be baptized, read the Bible daily, pray daily, publicly confess and witness for Christ, attend the church worship services and pay tithes.

Lesson 3
Power to Witness for Christ

I have read Acts 8-14: Yes _____ No _____

I have read John 6-10: Yes _____ No _____

MEMORIZE: Luke 13:3.

From previous studies you learned that since you had believed on and had received Christ as your Savior, God had given you power to become His son: "As many as received him (Jesus), to them gave he (God) power to become the sons of God, even to them that believe on his name" (John 1:12). Thus, receiving Christ gave you power to become God's son; now you need power to witness. Witnessing for and confessing Christ as one's Lord and Savior is one sign that a person is a Christian (1 John 4:13; Romans 10:9, 10).

You will note that the apostle Peter, for example, was saved, as were the other disciples of Christ (Luke 10:20), before the Day of Pentecost (a Jewish feast day) mentioned in Acts 2. He was among the first disciples who went forth to reach others for Christ (Matthew 10:1-7) and made at least two recorded open confessions of faith in Christ (Matthew 16:16; John 6:69). Yet Peter at times showed great weakness in his testimony for Jesus (Mark 14:67-71). However, on and after the Day of Pentecost, Peter preached and witnessed fearlessly (Acts 2:14; 4:7, 8; 10:34-43). When you accepted Christ, God gave you the power of sonship—power to witness to others of this salvation. Read the following questions; look up the Scripture references given. In your own words, write the answers.

I. PURPOSE OF BAPTISM (OUTPOURING, GIFT, FILLING) OF THE HOLY GHOST

A. What does the baptism of the Holy Ghost (Holy Spirit, Comforter) give one power to do (Acts 1:8)?

B. Whom will the Holy Ghost testify of when He enters the believer (John 15:26)?

C. In addition to empowering the believer for service, what two other things does the Holy Ghost do for the Christian (John 14:26)?

D. How does the Holy Ghost help the Christian in prayer (Romans 8:26)?

II. OUTPOURING OF THE HOLY GHOST FORE-TOLD

A. Foretold by Old Testament prophet—before the coming of the Messiah, Jesus Christ, the Holy Spirit was given primarily to the prophets and to the spiritual leaders of Israel. However, Joel, one of the minor prophets, prophesied that in the last days (the days since the resurrection of Christ) the Holy Ghost would be given to other people besides the prophets. Who were and are those on whom the Spirit was and is poured out? (Joel 2:28, 29; Acts 2:16-18)?

B. Foretold by John the Baptist—what was the difference between the baptism of John the Baptist and the baptism of Jesus (Mark 1:8; Matthew 3:11)?

C. Foretold by Christ—Jesus, in Acts 1:5, was the last to speak of the baptism of the Holy Ghost before the outpouring on the Jewish day of Pentecost. Who remembered these words of Christ later and what caused him to remember them (Acts 11:2, 15, 16)?

III. FULFILLMENT OF THE PROPHECY CONCERNING THE PROMISE OF THE BAPTISM OF THE HOLY GHOST

A. When the first believers were filled with the Holy Ghost in Acts 2:1-13 . . .

   1. In what city were they?

   2. On what day was it?

   3. What did the Christians do when they were filled with the Holy Ghost?

   4. What did the unbelievers and other onlookers think was wrong with the disciples?

B. Some time later, possibly a year or two following the Pentecostal outpouring, the Evangelist Philip had a successful revival at Samaria. What does the Bible specifically say happened to the believers following this revival (Acts 8:15-17)?

C. When Peter preached the gospel to the first Gentile congregation—at the house of Cornelius, the Roman Centurion, at Caesarea about 10 years after Pentecost, how did the Jews ("they of the circumcision"), who were with Peter, know that the Holy Ghost was poured out on these Gentiles (Acts 10:45, 46)?

D. Some 25 years after the first outpouring of the Holy Ghost at Jerusalem, Paul, on the final lap of his second missionary journey, found 12 disciples at Ephesus in Asia Minor. These disciples had heard John the Baptist's preaching about the coming Messiah, Jesus Christ; however, they had not yet heard about the baptism of the Holy Ghost. What did they do when the Holy Ghost came on them (Acts 19:6)?

E. Does one receive the baptism of the Holy Ghost at the time he is saved or does one always receive the gift of the Holy Ghost after an interval of some time (Acts 10:44; 19:1, 2)?

F. Is a person always baptized in water before receiving the Holy Ghost baptism (Acts 8:15-17; 10:44-48; 19:5, 6)?

IV. SPEAKING IN TONGUES FORETOLD

A. In Isaiah's prophecy concerning tongues, does he state that people will hear or reject it (Isaiah 28:11, 12)?

B. When the apostle Paul refers to this prophecy in Isaiah, for whom does he say that tongues are a sign (1 Corinthians 14:21, 22)?

C. Just before His ascension, Jesus stated that speaking with new tongues would be a sign which would follow certain people. Who would these people be (Mark 16:17)?

(Note to student: The term *speaking in (new, unknown or other) tongues* is used in the Bible in reference to the baptism of the Holy Spirit and in reference to the last two of the nine gifts of the Holy Spirit mentioned in 1 Corinthians

261

12:8-10. In either case, the term is used in association with a manifestation of the Holy Spirit of God.

In 1 Corinthians 14 the apostle Paul cautions the Corinthian church and gives its members advice with regard to the wise use of this spiritual gift. Paul states that one who prophesies edifies the church, whereas he that speaks in an unknown tongue edifies only himself. He states that one who prophesies is greater than one who speaks with tongues unless the latter can also interpret in order that the church may be edified (vv. 4, 5). Paul indicates that speaking to people in tongues without an interpreter is profitless (v. 6), is like giving an indistinct sound on a musical instrument (v. 7), is like an uncertain bugle command during battle (v. 8), is like speaking into the air (v. 9) is meaningless to the hearer (v. 11), and will cause the unlearned or the unbeliever to think that those whom they hear are mad (v. 23). Speaking in tongues with an interpreter however, according to Paul, is at least equal to the gift of prophecy (v. 5). Paul states further that in order to edify the church, one who speaks in an unknown tongue should also pray that he might interpret (v. 13); and the apostle gives instructions for the use of this gift during a church service: "If any man speak in an unknown tongue, let it be by two, or at the most by three, and that by course; and let one interpret" (v. 27).

You will note that these instructions from Paul deal with the use of this spiritual gift during a coming together of the believers for worship and instruction. He puts no limits on the use of this gift when the believer is in prayer in secret, at home, and after the regular instructional or preaching service is concluded at church. That Paul understood the spiritual meaning of this gift, desired that all

Christians possess it, possessed and used the gift to his own edification as well as the edification of others, knew that it was a sign from God, realized that it was a gift that would not be believed and accepted, and understood that Christians were to be permitted to speak with tongues is clear from the following verses in 1 Corinthians 14: "He that speaketh in an unknown tongue speaketh not unto men, but unto God" (v. 2); "I would that ye all spake with tongues, but rather that ye prophesied" (v. 5); "I will pray with the spirit . . . I will sing with the spirit" (v. 15); "I thank my God, I speak with tongues more than ye all" (v. 18); "Tongues are for a sign . . . to them that believe not" (v. 22); "With men of other tongues and other lips will I speak unto this people; and yet for all that will they not hear me, saith the Lord" (v. 21); "Wherefore, brethren, covet to prophesy, and forbid not to speak with tongues" (v. 39).

V. THOSE TO WHOM THE GIFT OF THE HOLY GHOST IS PROMISED

A. Peter's sermon on the Day of Pentecost names the people to whom the gift of the Holy Ghost is promised. Who are they and into which category do you fit? (Acts 2:38, 39)

B. What is one of the things a person must do in order to be given the Holy Ghost (Acts 5:32)?

C. What else may a person sometimes have to do before being endued with power from God through the outpouring of the Holy Ghost (Luke 24:49)?

D. Read Luke 11:5-13. Note especially verses 8 and 13. (The word *importunity* comes from a verb, *importune*, which is defined as: "to ply or press with requests; to urge persistently; to request or solicit with urgency"). The best you can, in your own words, point out at least one other condition or requirement that may have to be met before a person is filled with the Holy Ghost.

E. Read John 14:16, 17. (Note that Jesus promises the Holy Ghost as a comforter.) After reading the verses indicated, answer the following questions:

1. To whom is Jesus speaking?

2. Who will pray that the Holy Ghost be sent?

3. Who will send the Holy Ghost?

4. How long will the Comforter abide?

5. Why can the world (the unsaved, the sinners) not receive the Holy Spirit?

Review separately, Acts 16:31, 1 John 1:9, and Luke 13:3; close your Bible; then, from memory, recite these verses.

Remember you have already been born of the Spirit of God; therefore, you should begin to confess Christ as your Savior and to witness for Him. If you have not yet received the baptism of the Holy Ghost, which will give you great and greater power to serve and to witness for Christ, then begin now to be importunate and to ask the Lord for this promised Gift. Elisha asked of Elijah that he be granted a double portion of his spirit (see 2 Kings 2:9). After Elijah was taken away, this request was granted and Elisha performed twice as many miracles as had Elijah. God gave of His Holy Spirit to Jesus without measure and God's Son was victorious in every battle with the devil. The more you are filled with the Spirit of God, the more effective will be your endeavors to win souls for Jesus.

Between now and the time you receive Lesson 4, read Acts 15-21. Reading at the rate of at least one chapter per day, you will normally be able to finish the suggested number between lessons. If you read with greater than average speed and if you complete the reading assignment before receiving the next lesson, then read John 11-15.

Every Christian who desires to be a fruitful servant of the Savior, Jesus of Nazareth, should, if at all possible, do these things: be baptized, read the Bible daily, pray daily, publicly confess and witness for Christ, attend church worship services and pay tithes.

Lesson 4
The Coming of Christ and the Millennium

I have read Acts 15—21: Yes _____ No _____

I have read John 11—15: Yes _____ No _____

MEMORIZE: Romans 10:9.

The first coming of Christ was when He, in fulfillment of prophecy, was the promised Prophet and Messiah to the Jews (Deuteronomy 18:15; John 6:14), was born in Bethlehem (Micah 5:2; Matthew 2:1) of the Virgin Mary (Isaiah 7:14; Matthew 1:18), was rejected by the Jews (Isaiah 5:33; John 1:11), was crucified with sinners (Isaiah 53:12; Matthew 27:38), was resurrected (Psalm 16:10; Matthew 28:9), and ascended into heaven (Psalm 68:18; Luke 24:50, 51).

The next coming of Christ (the coming in the air) will be to catch away (rapture) His people to be with Him forever. After this, the Antichrist will come into power and the great tribulation will begin. The tribulation will last for a period of seven years, at the end of which Christ will return to earth again (the second coming of Christ) and will destroy the Antichrist and his kingdom, at which time the Jews will finally accept Christ as their Messiah. Following this, Christ will rule on earth for a period of 1,000 years (the Millennium); then there will be another great battle which will result in the bringing into subjection of all powers that oppose God. Read the following questions; look up the Scripture references given; and, in your own words, write the answers.

I. THE RAPTURE OF THE CHURCH

A. At the time of the Rapture, will Christ return to the earth for His people (1 Thessalonians 4:17)?

B. What will happen to the "dead in Christ" (vv. 13-16)?

C. What will happen to those who are alive "in Christ" (v. 17)?

D. What will happen to the bodies of all Christians at the sounding of the trumpet at the Rapture (1 Corinthians 15:51-53; Philippians 3:20, 21)?

E. To whom shall Christ appear at the time of His coming in the air (Hebrews 9:28)?

F. If we hope to meet Christ in the air at His appearing, how should we live (Titus 2:12, 13)?

G. What has Christ gone to prepare for those for whom He will return (John 14:1-3)?

H. According to the "Parable of the Pounds" (Luke 19:11-27), what should we as servants of the Lord do until He comes back for us (v. 13)?

I. What does the Christian receive from the knowledge that Christ will soon catch His people away (1 Thessalonians 4:18)?

J. After the Rapture, how long shall we be with the Lord (v. 17)?

II. THE GREAT TRIBULATION

A. After the Rapture and the church is "taken out of the way" (2 Thessalonians 2:7), the "Wicked" or

Antichrist will be revealed (v. 8). Where will the Antichrist get his working power (v. 9)?

B. What other names are given to the Antichrist (v. 3)?

C. How bad will the Great Tribulation be (Matthew 24:21)?

[Note: Revelation 6-19 covers the Tribulation period (seven years). You may read these chapters to get a picture of the awfulness of this period. God permits the Tribulation to come about in order to bring Israel, who has rejected the Messiah and has thus been left desolate, to repentance (Matthew 23:34-39).]

D. How can a person avoid going through the Great Tribulation? (Luke 21:36; Revelation 3:10)?

E. Of what great feast in heaven will the raptured Christians be partaking while the Tribulation is in progress on earth (19:9)?

III. THE SECOND COMING OF CHRIST

A. At the end of the seven-year tribulation period, who will return with Christ to earth (Jude 14; Matthew 16:27)?

B. What will be the purpose of the Lord's second coming to the earth (Jude 15; Matthew 16:27)?

C. Who alone knows the hour and day of Christ's second coming to the earth (Matthew 24:36)?

D. How does the present return of the Jews (children of Israel) to the Holy Land show that the second coming of the Lord cannot be too far in the future (Hosea 3:4, 5)?

E. What are some other signs that indicate we are living in the latter days (2 Timothy 3:1-5; 2 Peter 3:3, 4)

F. Will Christ be visible to people of the world at His second coming to earth (Revelation 1:7)?

G. What wounds in connection with His crucifixion will the people notice at Christ's return to earth (Zechariah 13:6)?

H. What will the people on earth do when they see the Lord returning to earth (Matthew 24:30)?

I. What is one of the specific spots on earth to which Christ will return (Zechariah 14:1-4)?

J. During Christ's second return, what will He do with the Antichrist (the Beast) and the False Prophet (Revelation 19:19, 20)?

K. On Christ's second return to earth, after the Jews have seen His nail-scarred hands (Zechariah 13:6) and after these Jews have been tried by fire (the Great Tribulation), will Christ have accomplished His purpose of bringing Israel (the Jews) to repentance (Zechariah 13:9)?

IV. THE MILLENNIUM

A. Immediately after the Tribulation, Christ begins His millennial reign. What happens to the devil during this reign (Revelation 20:1-3)?

B. What will be the titles of Christ during His millennial reign at Jerusalem (19:11-16)?

C. What will resurrected Christians do during this period (20:6)?

D. Will there be any war during the Millennium (Isaiah 2:4)?

E. Will there be prosperity or poverty during Christ's thousand-year reign (Ezekiel 36:30-35)?

F. What will be the temperament of normally wild animals and serpents during the Millennium (Isaiah 11:6-9)?

G. How much of the world will have the gospel during the millennial reign of Christ (v. 9)?

H. What is the great purpose of Christ's thousand-year reign on earth (1 Corinthians 15:24, 25)?

I. What does the devil do when released at the end of the Millennium (Revelation 20:7-9)?

J. What ultimately happens to the devil, the Beast (Antichrist), and the False Prophet (v. 10)?

K. After the Great Judgment, what happens to all those whose names are not found written in the Book of Life (vv. 11-15)?

L. Who will be permitted to enter the heavenly city, the "holy Jerusalem" of God (21:21-27)?

Review separately, Acts 16:31, 1 John 1:9, Luke 13:3, and Romans 10:9; close your Bible; then, from memory, write these verses.

Between now and the time you receive Lesson 5, read Acts 22—28. At the rate of one chapter per day, you will normally be able to finish the suggested number between lessons. If you read with greater than average speed and if you complete the reading of the Book of Acts before receiving the next lesson, then read John 16—21.

Every Christian who desires to be a fruitful servant of the Savior, Jesus of Nazareth, should, if at all possible, do these things: Be baptized, read the Bible daily, pray daily, publicly confess and witness for Christ, attend church worship services and pay tithes.

Lesson 5
Stewardship

I have read Acts 22-28: Yes _____ No _____
I have read John 16-21: Yes _____ No _____
MEMORIZE: Acts 1:8.

Stewardship is the act of a steward. A steward is presented in the Bible as one to whom something has been committed and one who is engaged in service for another. Christ has committed to us the witness of the gospel both by mouth and by example.

This lesson teaches about our stewardship of material (money and possessions) and spiritual (the gospel) which God has committed to us. Read the following questions; look up the Scripture references given; and, in your own words, write the answers in the spaces provided.

I. TITHE

The word *tithe* means one-tenth or a tenth part and has reference to the giving of one-tenth of our income to the work of the Lord.

A. To whom did Abraham pay tithe on one occasion (Hebrews 7:1, 2; Genesis 14:18-20)?

B. What was this man's position (Genesis 14:18)?

C. Was this before or after the Mosaic Law was given (the commandment to pay tithe was given in Leviticus 27:30.)?

D. Name another man who paid tithe to the Lord before the Mosaic Law was given (Genesis 28:16-22).

E. What then would be your reply to those who object to tithing on the basis that it is an old Mosaic Law which no longer needs to be obeyed?

F. How had the people robbed God (Malachi 3:8)?

G. What command and what promise concerning the tithe are given by God in Malachi 3:10?

H. When Jesus pronounced woe upon the scribes and Pharisees: 1. What weighty things did He say ought to be remembered? 2. In this same verse, what did He say ought not to be left undone (Matthew 23:23)?

I. Is there a difference made between paying tithes and giving offerings (Malachi 3:8)?

J. Offerings to God, other than the tithe, ought to be given according to what three rules (2 Corinthians 9 What kind of giver does God love (v. 7)?

II. GIVING TO THE NEEDY

A. What judgment is pronounced upon those who will not hear the cry of the poor (Proverbs 21:13)?

B. What promise is given to those who help the poor (14:21)?

C. What did Jesus say we ought to do when the needy ask for help (Matthew 5:42)? (It is up to each one of us to determine the need according to our conscience. Everyone who might ask for money does not especially come under the meaning of the needy.)

D. Read Acts 20:35.

1. Who did Paul say ought to be supported?

2. What words of Jesus did Paul quote in this verse?

3. Do you agree?

III. WITNESSING TO THE LOST

God has given us money so we may give our tithes and offerings. He has also given us money so we may give to the needy. But God has given us something far better than money which He expects us to give to others. That is the GOSPEL.

A. Why did God give His Son (John 3:16)?

B. What will happen to lost men and women if we do not give them the gospel so they may be saved (Revelation 20:10, 14, 15)?

C. Read Mark 16:15. This commandment is directed to all Christians, not just to those in the ministry. Any time the plan of salvation is given to lost people whether in church, on the street, in the jail or in the home, whether to one person or to many, the person giving the plan is preaching. Will you, with God's help, put forth an effort to witness for Christ to the lost?

D. To whom are we to preach the gospel (Mark 16:15)?

E. Where are we to preach the gospel (Mark 16:15)? Does this mean in homes, jails, and streets as well as in the church?

F. For what reason does God give the power of the Holy Ghost to Christians (Acts 1:8)?

G. What solemn warning does God give to His people (Ezekiel 3:17-21)?

H. What two ways do Christians overcome the devil (Revelation 12:11)?

I. What two conditions are we to meet in order to be saved (Romans 10:13, 14)?

Review separately, Acts 16:31, 1 John 1:9, Luke 13:3, Romans 10:9, and Acts 1:8; close your Bible; then, from memory, recite these verses.

You may now begin a systematic reading of the Bible. If you read three chapters each day and five chapters on Sunday, you will complete both the Old and New Testaments in one year. You have now read the Book of Acts and the Gospel of John. It is suggested that you next read Paul's Epistle to the Romans and follow this by reading the Book of Revelation. You may then read the remaining books of the New Testament. After this you should read the Old Testament, beginning with Genesis.

Every Christian who desires to be a fruitful servant of the Savior, Jesus of Nazareth, should, if at all possible, do these things: be baptized, read the Bible daily, pray daily, publicly confess and witness for Christ, attend church worship services and pay tithes.

BIBLE STUDY FOR CHILDREN

Lesson 1
Salvation

How do we become a Christian?

"If we confess our sins, he is faithful and just to forgive us our sins, and to cleanse us from all unrighteousness" (1 John 1:9).

We cannot always believe what people tell us, but we can believe what God has told us in the Bible. In the above scripture, we find that God tells us that if we tell Him about our sins and we are sorry for our sins, He will forgive us.

Did you know that if you had been the only lost person in the world, Jesus would have died for just you; and if you were the only person who confessed your sins, He would forgive you? But in His Word, He tells us that all of us have done things that are wrong or in other words, have sinned (read Romans 3:23).

What is salvation?

Now that you have asked Jesus to come into your heart, you have salvation. Maybe you do not know what salvation is. It is not just going to church and being good. Many people do good deeds and go to church who have never received salvation (read Ephesians 2:8, 9.) To receive true salvation, we must believe on Jesus and accept Him as our very own Savior (read Acts 16:31).

We often call salvation the new birth (read John 3:4-7). The first time we are born, we receive the natural life, and are born into our parents' family. Then, when we accept the Lord Jesus as our personal Savior, we are born into God's family and are called the children of God (read John 1:12).

What made it possible for us to have salvation?

Do you really realize what God did for you? Your mother and father would not let you die even for someone who loved you. But God let Jesus, His only Son, die for people who hated Him. He did this so that we might be saved (read John 3:16).

I once heard about a mother who tried to tell her son about what Jesus did for him, but he did not understand. One morning while he was playing outside, a bee got after him. The bee gave the little boy a big scare. He ran and ducked under his mother's apron. She put her arms around him, and the bee stung her on the face. After she felt the sting, she told the little boy to come out because the bee could not harm him. The little boy looked at the mother's swollen face while she explained to him that in a way, this was what Jesus had done for him. When He died on the cross, He bore the sting of sin for us all, and we do not have to pay for our sins. Isn't it wonderful that He loved us and took our place? It should have been us who had to suffer for our sins, but Jesus suffered and died for us. Yes, salvation is the most wonderful thing in all the world, and we have only to believe in Jesus to receive it.

Isn't Jesus wonderful? And don't you love Him with all your heart? I know you do! Do you know the little song titled, "I Love Him"? Let's sing it in the morning when we awaken; at noon, and in the evening before we go to bed. Let's mean it with all our heart.

I love Him, I love Him.

Because He first loved me.

And purchased my salvation,

On Calvary.

And let's not forget to read our Bible and pray every day, thanking God for this wonderful salvation. You see, once you were lost, and you did what Satan wanted you to do, but now, Jesus has found you and made you His child. He has adopted you into His family. And aren't you glad! Can you say aloud, "Jesus, I thank You for saving my soul?" Now, don't you feel better? There is a little song that says the same thing. We ought to sing it often. It will help us to grow and become strong Christians. It goes like this:

Thank You Lord, for saving my soul.

Thank You, Lord, for making me whole.

Thank You, Lord, for giving to me,

Thy great salvation, so full and free.

If you don't know the tune, then memorize it and say it at least once every day. See if it doesn't help you to be a better Christian.

279

QUESTIONS

1. Tell in your own words what the following scriptures mean to you:
   a. 1 John 1:9
   b. Ephesians 2:8, 9
   c. John 3:16
2. How can we get Jesus to forgive us of our sins?
3. What is meant by the "new birth"?
4. By using the story about the bee, tell us what Jesus did for you.
5. Tell us when and how you received salvation.

Lesson 2
Daily Devotions

The Christian life is a fight!

Many people think the Christian's life is easy. They think that after they are saved, there will be no difficulties. But the Christian's life is full of temptations and difficulties, because we are in a battle against the devil, who is the enemy of God's children.

We must stay in touch with God!

We must always be in touch with the Lord, because we are not strong enough in our own selves to defeat Satan. We overcome the Enemy's power by praying and reading God's Word, the Bible. When we pray, we talk to God; and when we read the Bible, God talks to us.

The Bible is God-breathed!

The Word of God is a God-inspired book. Second Timothy 3:16 tells us that "all scripture is given by inspiration of God." *Inspiration of God* comes from one word in the Greek language which means "God breathed." Isn't that wonderful? The Bible had 40 different writers, but God told everyone of those writers just what to write. Many people have tried to destroy the Bible, but God has kept it through the years. Isaiah 40:8 says, "The word of our God shall stand for ever."

The Bible meets all of our needs.

The Word of God answers life's greatest questions. It tells us all we know about God; it tells us where we came from and where we are going; it tells us how to be saved and how to live holy. In fact, the Bible discusses nearly every other important subject. God speaks to people's hearts daily through the Bible and they are saved.

When Satan hears the Bible read or quoted, he flees faster than the fastest horse in a race, because he hates God's Word. When Jesus was tempted by Satan In the wilderness, He repeated God's Word. In this way, Jesus defeated Satan, and Satan fled (read Matthew 4:1-11). It works that way today also.

The Bible is like a mirror because it shows us how we look. As we read the Bible, we can see the wrong things in our lives. But the Bible is better than a mirror because in it we also find a way to correct the wrong and to replace the ugliness in our lives with beauty.

We are cleansed as we read God's Word, because as we fill our minds and hearts with the Word of God, it crowds out those things that are not clean.

The Bible is a sword. The Enemy is holding some of your best friends in his prison of sin right now. They are lost and condemned to death. Ephesians 6:17 tells us that the Word of God is the sword of the Spirit. We can use this sword to defeat Satan and to set our friends free.

So let's study our Bibles; let's use it to fight the devil and to win others to Christ.

Our God answers prayer.

Many people pray. Some people pray to gods of wood; some people pray to Gods of clay; some people pray to gods of stone. We know that these gods cannot answer prayer, but our heavenly Father *hears* and *answers* prayer.

You know, many people think that to pray means to ask God for things—so, they ask Him for all sorts of silly, unnecessary things. But the Bible tells us, ". . . your Father knoweth what things you have need of, before ye ask him" (Matthew 6:8). And the very next verses tell us how to pray: "After this manner therefore pray ye: Our Father which art in heaven, Hallowed be thy name. . . ." (Look up this scripture and read the rest of this prayer (vv. 9-13).)

We need to pray and thank God for saving us. We need to pray and let Him know we love Him, that we desire to live for Him and please Him. We need to pray for those who are lost in sin that they might be saved. We need to pray for our missionaries, preachers, Sunday school teachers, and our friends who are also Christians. We need to pray that the Lord will keep us safe from the devil and to say no when we are tempted to do wrong. We need to pray for the leaders of our country that God will help them and give them wisdom to do the right things and make the right decisions.

We have a lot to pray about, don't we? And as you pray, you will think of many other things that need praying about.

When we are sick, worried, feeling blue, let us slip away and talk to God. Let us remember John 3:16. (Read it. Or if you know it, say it aloud.) Then read Romans 8:32. What does this scripture say God will freely give us? Yes, "all things." And that means all things that we need to be happy, glowing and growing Christians. Isn't the Lord wonderful? Don't you love Him a whole lot? I know you do.

How to Pray

Many people think you can pray only on your knees; others feel you can only pray standing up. But God's Word tells us in 1 Thessalonians 5:17, to "Pray without ceasing." This means "pray without stopping." Pray while you are walking; pray while you're alone; and when you're

283

with others, *think* your prayers, without saying them aloud. God knows what we *think*. And oh, how much it pleases Him when we *think* about Him.

We grow in the Lord and the Word of God.

Did you know that through praying and reading God's Word, you can become a strong Christian? The more a Christian prays and reads his Bible, the more he is able to feel the presence of the Lord all warm and bubbling in his heart—and he just "shines" he is so happy. That is the kind of Christian we want to be, isn't it?

So let's pray and read God's Word every day and shine for Him.

QUESTIONS

1. Why must we always be in contact with God?
2. How do we overcome the Enemy's power?
3. What is prayer?
4. What does *inspiration of God* mean?
5. How many different writers did the Bible have?
6. Write out Isaiah 40:8.
7. List at least five of the many things that the Bible answers for us or does for us.
8. How is the Bible like a mirror?
9. How is the Bible like a sword?
10. Write out Matthew 7:7, 8, 11.

Lesson 3
A Closer Walk With God

How should we love God?

Did you ever stop to think about how big God is? Look around you someday as you're playing outdoors. Everything you see—the trees, the sun, the grass, the flowers—God made them. What? You see a house and an automobile, and you do not believe God made them? Just one moment, please! Let us think. Who made the materials man used to build the house and the auto? God did! Because God made the whole earth. And He made you too.

Yes, this is the same God who sent His only Son, Jesus, to die on the ugly, rugged cross on Mount Calvary so that your sins and mine could all be taken away so that you could live with Him forever in a lovely place called heaven. Did you know the Bible says that God doesn't want anybody to be lost and go to hell? (Read 2 Peter 3:9.) The more we learn about God, the more we love Him. He is so wonderful! And He loves us more than we can ever possibly love Him. Do you know what the first and greatest commandment is? It commands us to love God. Read Matthew 22:37 to learn how God wants us to love Him. Now think! Do you love God the way He wants you to love Him? Let's pause right now and bow our heads and pray that God will help us to love and trust Him more:

"Dear heavenly Father, I thank You for sending Your Son, Jesus, to die that I might be saved. And when I look round about me and see all the lovely things You have made for me to enjoy, I love and appreciate You so much. But Father, You've told me in Your Word, the Bible, 'Thou shalt love the Lord thy God with all thy heart, and with all thy soul, and with all thy mind.' And I am not sure that I do. Will you help me to love You more and draw me closer to You? Thank You, in Jesus' name. Amen."

Ah! Now don't you feel better? Don't you love to talk to God? He made us a wonderful promise in James 4:8. (Read it.) What does the Bible say God will do if we will draw nigh (near) to Him?

What kind of Christian do you want to be?

Did you know there are two kinds of Christians? One kind goes to church on Sunday and prays every night before he goes to bed and tries to find time to read his Bible. The other kind of Christian asks God to help him to be the best Christian he can possibly be—moment by moment, every day. He wants even his thoughts to please God. One man in the Bible, whose name is David, wanted to be this kind of Christian. Turn in your Bible to Psalm 19:14 and read the prayer David prayed. The word *meditations* means "thoughts."

Do you want your thoughts—everything you think, and words—everything you say, and deeds—everything you do, to please God? I know you do! But if everything we think, say or do pleases God, then there are two things especially that we must do every day: (1) We must read God's Word, the Bible, and learn His commandments, and read and study those things He has told us to do and those things He has told us not to do. (2) We must pray every day that God will guide us and help us to do, say and think those things that would please Him. Let us pray the prayer that David prayed right now. All right? "Let the words of my mouth, and the meditation of my heart, be acceptable in thy sight, O Lord, my strength, and my redeemer" (v. 14).

Yes, we want to be the best Christian we can possibly be, don't we? And if we but ask Him, Jesus will live in our hearts so much that others will be able to see Him in us—in the way we work and play; in the way we talk; in the way we treat our family and friends; and in everything we do. Aren't you glad you have Jesus living in your heart? I know you want to be as much like Him as you can possibly be.

How can we be real Christians every minute of the day?

It takes someone with a real backbone to serve Christ. Did you know that? Anybody can do what he "feels like" doing. Just anybody can tell a lie when he finds he is in trouble. Anybody can take something that doesn't belong to him, just because he wishes it were his. Anyone can get angry and throw a tantrum. But it takes a really brave and strong person to live for Jesus, to read His Word and to do what God says to do, regardless of what others may do—to pray every day and to let the beauty of Jesus shine through him or her.

We can live for Jesus and be real Christians every minute of the day if we:

1. Purpose in our heart (make up our mind) to live for Jesus and please Him, come what may.

2. Pray every day for God to forgive us for our mistakes and help us to do better.

3. Read God's Word and memorize parts of it.

4. Tell others how wonderful Jesus is, and that they need to accept Him as their Savior, too.

5. Believe that Jesus will hold our hand and walk beside us at all times and help us to be real Christians.

   Aren't you glad you know Jesus?

QUESTIONS

1. Who made the beautiful stars, moon, sun, grass, trees and flowers?

2. Who does the Bible say loved the world (you and me) so much that He sent His only Son to die for us (John 3:16)?

3. Whom doesn't God want to perish (be lost)? Read 2 Peter 3:9 and write this Scripture, beginning with the words, "not willing."

4. What is the first and greatest commandment? Write it. (Matthew 22:39)

5. What does God say He will do if we will draw nigh (near) unto Him? (James 4:8, Answer in your own words.)

6. After reading David's prayer in Psalm 19:14, what kind of Christian do you think he was? Do you think he pleased God? (Read Acts 13:22.)

7. What does the word *meditations* mean?

8. What two things must we do every day if we want our thoughts to please God?

9. List five things we must do each day if we are to be real Christians and please God.

10. Tell in your own words how living for Jesus has caused you to be different. (Are you happier?)

Do your friends notice a change in you? When you're tempted to do something wrong, do you feel Jesus beside you, helping you to be strong? Do you realize that you are a child of God, that God is your heavenly Father, and that He loves you very much and is watching over you every minute of every day?

Every day with Jesus is sweeter than the day before.

Every day with Jesus, I love Him more and more.

Jesus saves and keeps me, and He's the One I'm waiting for.

Every day with Jesus is sweeter than the day before.

Lesson 4
Tell Others About Jesus

What We Talk About

When we love someone, we usually say we love him/her with all our heart. Have you ever heard anyone say, "I love him with all my heart"? The Bible says we talk about whatever is in our heart (see Matthew 12:34). The word *abundance* means an "overflowing fullness" or "great plenty." The Scripture really means, "From all thoughts stored up in the heart, the mouth chooses what it talks about."

What God Wants Us to Talk About

In lesson 3 you learned the first commandment. Do you remember what it is? In case you cannot remember, look it up again (Deuteronomy 6:5). You see, God wants us to love Him "with all our heart." If we love God this much, do you suppose we will ever mention Him when we talk to our friends and our family? How do you know? (Read Matthew 12:34 again.) That is right. When Jesus lives in our heart, we just cannot help but tell others about how wonderful He is. We who know Jesus and know that He lives in our hearts love to read the Bible (because the Bible is God's love letter to us), and we love to pray (because when we pray, we are talking to God). We love to tell others about Him, because we want to do what He tells us to do in His Word, the Bible. And He has told us to witness. The word *witness* means "to tell someone else something you know to be true." We know that Jesus can save sinners, don't we? How do we know? We know, because He has saved us!

Four Things God Wants Us to Tell Others

In the Bible God tells us some things He expects us to talk about to our friends and neighbors—and to everyone who does not know Him:

1. He wants us to tell them that everyone needs to be saved: I, you and they (read Romans 3:23).

2. He wants us to tell them they cannot save themselves. Many people think that by trying to be as good as they can, they can save themselves—but let's you and me see what the Bible says (read Titus 3:5 and Zechariah 4:6). These Scriptures mean that good deeds will not and cannot save us. Because He loves us and has mercy upon us (or feels sorry for us), Jesus can and will save us. We are helpless to save ourselves, but Jesus can and will do it for us if we will but ask Him (read 1 John 1:9.)

3. God wants us to tell others that Jesus has already made a way for them to be saved, and that all they have to do is to accept it. Jesus died in our place on the cross of Calvary. He was nailed to the cross and bled and died there for your sins and mine. Do you know why God let Jesus do this? (Read John 3:16.) Right before He died, Jesus said, "It is finished" (see John 19:30). And it was finished. Jesus had finished making a way for you and me and all our friends and neighbors, and everybody in the whole world to be saved. We can do nothing to save ourselves but accept the way Jesus has made for us, and God wants us to tell others about this way.

4. God wants us to explain to others about the way Jesus has made. There are some things we must do before we can be saved. Many people do not know how to become a Christian. God wants us to tell them.

First of all, we must *believe* (read Acts 16:31 and Hebrews 11:6). *Diligently* means with "all your heart." We know that when a person seeks God with all his heart, God will reward that person, or in other words, give him something—salvation, or whatever he might need.

Second, we must *repent* (read Luke 13:3). Do you think, after reading that scripture, that it is important that everyone repent? Of course, it is important that everyone repent, isn't it? We do not want anyone to perish (die), do we? Do you remember what 2 Peter 3:9 says? (Read it—this Scripture tells us whom God wants to perish.) Does He want anyone to perish? No! He wants you and me to tell others that they need to repent. *Repent* means to "turn away from our sins," to say, "Lord, I'm sorry I have done things that have displeased You; and if You will help me, I will never do them again."

Third, we need to *confess our sins to God* (read 1 John 1:9). After we believe, repent (turn away from our sins), and confess our sins to God, there is yet one thing more that we must do: that is to "confess [Christ] before men" (Matthew 10:32). This means to tell others what Christ has done for us and that He is the Son of God. (Read Romans 10:9, 10.) We must confess with our "mouth," the Scripture says. If we do this, someone is sure to hear us, and then he will want to know Jesus too.

Did you know that God expects us to tell others about Him? (Read Matthew 10:32, 33.) I want Jesus to tell the Father about me, don't you? If this is what we really want then we must tell others about Him. That is what the Scripture says.

QUESTIONS

1. Look up Matthew 12:34. Write it. Explain it.

2. What does *abundance* mean?

3. What is the first commandment? If we really love God the way God wants us to love Him, how will it change what we talk about? Will it make us talk about God? Why?

4. What does the word *witness* mean?

5. What are the four things God wants us to tell others (especially those who do not know Him)? List them.

6. What three things must a person do to be saved? List them with Scriptures.

7. How do you know Jesus expects us to tell others about Him (Matthew 10:32, 33)? Explain in your own words.

8. Are you going to tell your friends, family and neighbors about your wonderful Friend, Jesus?

Lesson 5
Fruit of the Spirit

How do people know about Christ?

The Lord Jesus says in John 15:5, "I am the vine, ye are the branches: He that abideth in me, and I in him, the same bringeth forth much fruit: for without me ye can do nothing." The only way a vine can give fruit is through its branches. And the only way the world can ever really know what Jesus is like is through the lives of Christians who live close to Him and obey Him.

What kind of fruit does a Christian bear?

Galatians 5:22, 23 tells us that, "the fruit of the Spirit is love, joy, peace, longsuffering, gentleness, goodness, faith, meekness, temperance." As we learn what each of these aspects of the fruits of the Spirit is, let us examine our own lives. And let us pray that God will help us to be real fruit-bearing Christians.

What is love?

This is the first fruit the Bible mentions. Jesus said, "By this shall all men know that ye are my disciples, if ye have love one to another" (John 13:35). Love causes us to smile at people. Love causes us to help others when they are in need. Love makes us pleasant. Let us pray together right now:

"Lord, give me more love—help me to love You more. Help me to love my neighbor more, and those who are lost that I might be able to win them for You. Give me love in my heart and let it shine through, so that others may know that I am Your disciple. In Jesus' name. Amen."

What is joy?

What do you think about when you think of joy? Do you think of someone laughing, clapping his hands and jumping up and down? Some people do act like that when their hearts are full of joy. Others just smile real big and look happy. But when your heart is full of joy, it shows in your face and your actions. The apostle Paul said, talking about salvation, "Ye rejoice with joy unspeakable and full of glory" (1 Peter 1:8). If we have the fruit called love in our life, then joy just naturally grows along beside it. When we love the Lord and everyone around us, we do things to try to please them, and that brings joy. The following formula explains joy.

Jesus first
Others second
Yourself last

What is peace?

Peace is a quiet, calm feeling inside. A person who has the fruit of peace does not get upset easily. He does not scream and cry and pull his hair when things go wrong. No matter how upsetting things may become around us, the Bible says, "Thou wilt keep him in perfect peace, whose mind is stayed on thee: because he trusteth in thee" (Isaiah 26:3). Do you understand how to have the fruit of peace? This scripture says that if we think about the Lord and keep Him in our mind, heart and life, and trust Him to work everything out for the best, we will not get easily upset. We will have the fruit of peace.

What is longsuffering?

Some people are so touchy you are almost afraid to look at them closely. This fruit called longsuffering helps

Christians smile and be sweet, even when they are being done wrong. That is what *longsuffering* means—to be patient and smile, even when everything is going wrong. Our heavenly Father is pleased when He sees this fruit in our lives. Jesus tells us how to act in the fifth chapter of Matthew. Read the entire chapter.

What is gentleness?

Gentleness is "kindness." It is the result of love, joy, peace and longsuffering. Gentleness causes us to speak softly and sweetly. People like to be around those who are gentle, because they know the gentle person won't say harsh things to hurt their feelings. When the gentle person sees someone who is upset or discouraged, he will speak kindly to him and offer to help. God wants His children to be gentle and kind.

What is goodness?

The fruit of goodness, even more than the other aspects of fruit of the Spirit, comes as we pray and ask the Lord to live within us. Because it is Jesus living in our hearts that causes us to be good—to obey our parents, to be helpful, to be sweet, kind and gentle at all times—it is Jesus who causes us to help others. As we do good to others, they can see Christ in us. After we are saved, we need to pray, "Lord, help me to have the fruit of 'goodness' in my life so that others can see You in me." Doing good deeds will not save us, but after we are saved, we will do good deeds (read Ephesians 2:8, 9).

What is faith?

Faith is believing God will do what He says He will do. The way we got saved was by believing God would do what He said He would do (Read 1 John 1:9). We confessed our sins, believing the Lord would forgive us. That is faith. All of us have faith, but we need to use it. Would you like to have more faith? (Read Romans 10:17.) Now do you know how we can have more faith? This Scripture says our faith grows by listening to the preacher and reading the Bible.

What is meekness?

Meekness is "not fighting back"; it is "not returning evil for evil." The Bible says that Moses was the meekest man who ever lived. Moses was reared in a king's palace by the king's daughter, but he never acted like a stubborn mule when others seemed to be pushing him around. To be a good Christian—one that pleases God—we must be willing to be pushed around once in a while. Read Matthew 27, Mark 15, Luke 23 and John 19, and notice how Jesus reacted when His enemies mistreated Him. He expects us to be like Him. And the Bible says that even when they spit on Him, plucked out His beard and placed a crown of thorns on His brow, He opened not His mouth. We need to pray that the Lord will help us to be more like Him.

What is temperance?

The Lord wants us to be well-balanced Christians. He does not want us to be too much one way or another. He does not want us to talk too much, eat too much, play too much, or work too much. When the fruit called temperance is present in our lives, we say "no" when friends would try to get us to do things that would displease the Lord. And temperance also causes us to eagerly say "yes" when we see an opportunity to do good.

How can we grow fruit?

We must pray—stay close to God. Ask Him to walk with us every day and to teach you *His* will and *His* ways. When we study God's Word and ask Him to help us be fruit-bearing Christians . . . He will! Jesus said, "And all things, whatsoever ye shall ask in prayer, believing, ye shall receive" (Matthew 21:22). Let us pray together.

"Dear heavenly Father, search my heart and help me to empty it of all selfishness, pride, envy, and those things that are displeasing to You. Then, fill my heart, mind and life with love, joy, peace, longsuffering, gentleness, goodness, faith, meekness, and temperance, that I might be truly like You and that others might see and know that I am a Christian. In Jesus' name. Amen."

QUESTIONS

1. Memorize and write out Galatians 5:22, 23.
2. Memorize and write out John 15:9.
3. Tell in your own words what love is.
4. How can we have joy?
5. What is meant by the fruit longsuffering?
6. Tell some things that you can do to show goodness to others.
7. What is meant by temperance?
8. How can Christians grow fruit?
9. Write out Ephesians 2:8, 9.
10. Explain Matthew 5:9.